ONE MORE RIDE:

ONE MORE DAY TO TOUCH ONE MORE LIFE

ONE
— MORE —
RIDE

One More Day
to Touch One More Life

Presented by

Tom Montgomery

This is a work of creative nonfiction. The events are portrayed to the best of Thomas Montgomery's memory. While all the stories in this book are true, some names and identifying details have been changed to protect the privacy of the people involved. Any resulting resemblance to persons living or dead is entirely coincidental and unintentional.

Edited by Susan Sparks

Front cover and book design by DPWN Publishing

Published by DPWN Publishing
A division of the Dynamic Professional Women's Network, Inc.
1879 N. Neltnor Blvd. #316, West Chicago, IL 60185
www.OurDPWN.com

Printed in the United States of America

ISBN: 978-1-939794-16-1

What people are saying about Tom Montgomery's *One More Ride*:

"As a former police officer and now serving as a Chaplain, I can testify that life can become overwhelming without warning. There always is someone hurting and in need of comfort. One More Ride is a true look into the life of a servant of God, as he (with feet of clay) ministers in the name of Jesus. Climb on with Tom and take One More Ride into the front lines of service to God."

—Don Mansfield BCBS
Director of Chaplaincy/Senior Advocate
Family Courts

"Tom is one of those rare individuals who is present for people during their most difficult times. This great book captures just a few instances, where Tom's warmth and wisdom made a big difference in the lives of others."

—Joe Buzzello, Author, *The CAP Equation & Drawing Circles*

"Much thought and a great number of books have addressed the question, "Is there life after death?" Tom Montgomery's book takes on the more salient question: "Is there life before death?" Tom, a man of faith and compassion, tells how he's learning to live life all the way to the end, through taking "just one more ride." Although he refers to his long-time practice of riding with police officers on their patrols into often tragic and dangerous situations, the book is a carefully crafted allegory about choosing to live life on purpose despite difficulties, detours and ambiguities. He introduces us to good and great people, some of whom he has known and others he has read. These inspire us to take one more ride in the interests of someone we encounter who is hurting. Tom is inviting us to take that ride with him. I, for one, am climbing on."

—Mike Brown
Juvenile Chaplain

"We're not in Heaven yet. We're still negotiating the life we're living. Yet we embody a hope that makes it all worthwhile. Jesus looked over a hillside full of followers, expressed his understandings of their struggles and God's good will toward them in the Beatitudes. Then he told the spiritually impoverished crowd something remarkable, "You are the light of the world." Tom Montgomery believes this. He knows the fragility of his own heart, and he's learned to trust the Light that shines through its many cracks—as do so many of us he has befriended along the way. Thanks for not stopping short, Tom!"

—Tommy Jordan
Executive Director
New Day Program

"Some books teach you things. Some books touch your heart. One More Ride: One more Day to Touch One More Life is one of those great books that does both. First responders have always been amazing to me. They charge toward danger, instead of running away. Tom Montgomery is a "first responder to the soul." He is courageous and truly one of my heroes.

—Jeff C. West, Author of the Award-Winning Sales Fable,
The Unexpected Tour Guide

"Some situations take our breath away. Others pierce our hearts, leaving scars long afterward. This book is full of such events. However, in each instance of heartbreak, the helper embodies healing. He cradles the broken hearts and carries a piece of the burden as long as he can, then he moves on to the next case. He brings hope and reminds others of the Great Healer. And through the despair, we see light."

—Kelli Levey Reynolds
Writer, Reader, Believer

Introduction

Are there meaningful ways to comfort a person whose world has been rocked with bad news? Paul referred to God as the "source of all comfort." (2 Corinthians 1:3) Are we prone to leave it there or take it a step further where Paul took it? "He comforts us in all our troubles so that we can comfort others. When they are troubled, we will be able to give them the same comfort God has given us." (Verse 4)

"You only live once. But if you do it right, once is enough." —Mae West

I've always wanted to do it right, but handling hardship created a challenge. Family members and classmates passed from this life, as far back as I can remember. The passing of time has not made it easier.

I have reached a place in life, where I desperately want to give as effectively as I have received. Isn't that scriptural? "It's more blessed to give than to receive." Those words are not found in the account of Jesus's ministry, but Paul told the Ephesian elders Jesus spoke them (Acts 20:35) and that is good enough for me. Results are seldom obvious—at least immediately. There is no scorecard in this arena. Think of the givers you know. Is that their sweet spot or what?

The golf term "sweet spot" is used here to identify a person's calling or purpose—including mine. Many people go their entire lives and never find their sweet spot. Long ago, I resolved not to be one of them. Although I am in the back nine of my life, I am convinced that I have found my sweet spot. I am not finished, and I want to go out on the move. However, it has come the hard way.

Gilda Radner wrote: "I wanted a perfect ending. Now I've learned the hard way, that some poems don't rhyme and some stories don't have a clear beginning, middle, and end. Life is about not knowing, having to change, taking the moment and making the best of it, without knowing what's going to happen next. Delicious Ambiguity."

After training for the ministry and serving there for a time, a life in sales occupied my next 40 years. Please be certain of one thing: I NEVER LEFT THE MINISTRY! One treasure in my library is an autographed collection of books by Og Mandino. He signed them in my presence and shook my hand. Every Zig Ziglar book was read, along with Norman Vincent Peal, Clement Stone and a constant flow of mentors (personally and in written form) who encouraged and motivated me. It is not only in a sales career, that motivation is needed. It is anywhere a person wishes to be his best.

Three principles are derived from those who have the gift of motivation:

1. Believe in ourselves

2. See value in what we do

3. Reject slavery to fear

This book is a collection of experiences that have shaped me—an outgrowth of a journal over time. Although each experience recorded was real, there has been an effort to make people and places as ambiguous as possible. My own identity cannot be disguised. It really was me—walking into heart-wrenching situations behind my heavenly Father who provided the words and guided the emotions of a willing son.

I love the book *Push the Rock* by R.W. Long. On page 36, he begins the chapter with a quote from Louis Zamperini, "Yet a part of you still believes you can fight and survive no matter what your mind knows. It's not so strange. Where there's still life, there's still hope. What happens is up to God."

Early on, Louis Zamperini was a juvenile delinquent. He took up running in high school, was a prisoner of war during WW2, a qualifier for the US in the 5000m race in the 1936 Berlin Olympics and became a Christian evangelist.

One cannot help but notice the instances in this record of depending on God for results. Many of the experiences faced involve cumulative stress, which multiplies the intensity of the pain. Ministering by being present is referred to in a discussion of the life and wisdom of Fred Rogers. Job's friends sat with him for seven days without saying a word. Silent presence alone has been a frequent ally and has a way of preventing us from coming away feeling unqualified and useless.

Proverbs 2:20 instructs us to "walk in the steps of good men." I have been blessed by many "good men" (and women) in my life. You will meet some of them. I now want to "pay it forward" and be that for others. Karl Jung wrote, "Be the man through whom you wish to influence others." I hope what is written will reveal my passion to do so.

This effort is dedicated first to my patient and understanding wife of more than 50 years. I have spent much of my life not knowing what I wanted to do "when I grow up." Brenda always has supported and believed in me. Dealing with uncertainties is something she does well.

Our three children (Holly Tomm, Paul Thomas, and Elizabeth Amber) have stuck with Dad when he was floundering, completely relying on faith and the support of their mom.

It would be negligence to ignore Mother and Dad (his life was not a waste), older sister Betty and her late husband Jimmie, younger sister Judy (my struggling companion growing up) and my deceased brother Dr. Robert Jr. and his wife Sandra (also deceased), who pointed me in the right direction when I had no direction of my own.

It is certainly appropriate to include the men and women who serve as first responders in my city (and everywhere). The work they do is a special calling. (Romans 13:1–3) I refer to them as my "post-graduate professors." Most of those who take me with them, are younger than my own children (sometimes grandchildren). At the end of the shift, each receives a "thank you" for what they have given and continue to give. They are my heroes.

I borrow a phrase from R.W. Long in the prologue to his book. "I went forward into the darkness." I have grown accustomed to living that way. In every case, God is found in the darkness and He is good. That is my message to the hurting. Would you join me?

Tom Montgomery

Preface

Seek Him First — Overcoming Me

It probably began, as I stood watching my Harley loaded onto a large trailer after the man had handed me a check. This was the culmination of over 65 years of motorcycle riding. Of all the things I have done in my life to gratify my cravings, riding a motorcycle was at the top. The Harley was a lifetime dream.

I've outgrown golf. A nice set of clubs sits in the garage, but it is difficult to justify spending four and a half hours out of a day doing something I never did well. I gave away most of the fishing gear. I have three full cases of shotgun shells for bird hunting.

I don't feel cheated at all. There are good memories from all these activities. One of my hunting friends hired a photographer and I have a CD of a pheasant hunting trip in South Dakota. I took my son on the last trip and it was worth every penny spent.

I read Mark 10:29–31 with new understanding. "I assure you that everyone who has given up house or brothers or sisters or mother or father or children or property, for my sake and for the Good News, will receive in return a hundred times as many houses, brothers, sisters, mothers, children, and property—along with persecution. And in the world to come that person will have eternal life."

Then there is Mark 8:36: "If you try to hang on to your life, you will lose it. But if you give up your life for my sake and for the sake of the good news, you will save it."

I must admit that many of the above qualify as self-indulgence. In all honesty, I cannot make a universal case against any of them. Even golf served a purpose, at times. I played in fundraisers, business development events meeting new people and even family activity. A while after retiring, I played while Brenda drove the cart. We usually would take our grandson along with an extra set of clubs and let him hit a few shots. He loved it and we loved being with him.

We spent two years caring for Brenda's mother during her cancer. We would rise early on Saturday, take a ride on our motorcycle, leaving mom to sleep in. Weeks were stressful and a bike ride was a good relief. The Harley was still in view. I've wanted one since I was a child.

I took my other bike to a dealer on a Saturday and came home with a Harley. The first thing Brenda did when she sat on it, was burn her leg on the exhaust (a common injury). After all the years riding and age setting in, I was feeling a little uneasy about putting my wife on the back. It was a dream come true with solo riding (other than a grandchild or two). Then Brenda got sick and I began taking blood thinning medicine. The bike had to go. I felt a little regret and grief, but I needed to make that transition. I need to be seeking hobbies and activities that glorify our long relationship—not divide it.

It is a bit of a letdown to read an obituary telling the life story of a man who was involved in everything but family. I read of how much value the person placed on hunting, fishing, motorcycles, auto racing or a certain football team. Not a single word about how much dedication was given to children and grandchildren. Those are the things that leave legacies. I have not done it perfectly, but my children and grandchildren have memories (along with pictures) of precious moments we spent together. Children need those more than I need a Harley.

I conduct a lot of funerals. Most of these are for people I never knew. I speak to the nearest relative and receive insight into the person's life. My remarks are centered on the unique things about that person and the impact he/

she made on those closest to them. Most of those things are taken for granted during their lifetime. It is my goal to send them away with reflections on the contribution that person made to the family.

Everyone has a purpose. Everyone comes into the world for a reason. "You made all the delicate, inner parts of my body and knit me together in my mother's womb." (Psalms 139:13)

Reaching even one more person, gives me reason to take one more ride.

Table of Contents

Chapter 1

What's so Special About Me?

*"I have become all things to all people so that by all
possible means I might save some. I do all this for the sake of the
gospel, that I may share in its blessings."* —1 Cor 9: 22–23

Can someone explain to me what makes a minister more special than anyone else? The Apostle Paul wrote that "he became all things to all people that he might save some." Is that only a goal for ministers? Paul's education or status alone did not make him effective in the lives of others.

Throughout my undergraduate and graduate training, never once did anyone instruct me on how to intervene at the point of tragedy in a person's life. There were no classes on "crisis intervention" and we never were directed to any kind of textbook or reading assignments on the subject. It is unlikely that academia ever will provide this skill. Even with the hours of classes I've taken in Crisis Intervention since college, situations are so unpredictable I find that faith supersedes skill.

I have the privilege of working closely with the police department, in the city where I grew up. The Clergy and Police Alliance (CAPA) is an effort to partner with the spiritual leaders of the community and communicate with those under their care. Church members need to be aware of what life is like beyond the church walls. We are called to the scene, when special intervention is needed. We are encouraged to ride as much of a ten-hour shift in a patrol car as our schedules will allow, experiencing what the officer experiences during his day. Ninety percent of the time we flow quietly through the city creating a police presence. Ten percent of the time we fly through intersections and traffic, with lights flashing and siren blaring. These officers are trained and skilled at handling their vehicles like a race car driver.

In many cases, the officer and I have only a fraction of the details. The dispatcher only can tell the officer what the caller tells him/her. We know we are about to encounter someone experiencing trauma—whether real or imagined. On the way to the scene, I beg God for the appropriate words and the heart to reach out with comfort.

What Are the words?

What does a minister say to a grandmother who has checked on her sleeping teenage granddaughter and found her deceased? She and her husband were rearing this young girl and her siblings.

Where do I find the words for a wife who has found her husband dead on the living room floor? He was watching television when she told him "good night" just a few hours before. And what about his son who gave me a hopeless look and said, "I didn't even get to tell him goodbye." The fishing boat in the driveway was my clue. "Did you fish a lot with your dad?" I asked.

"Oh yes, but now what am I going to do?"

Where are the words for a wife who shares children with her husband? Stress of unemployment and job rejection had taken their toll. She drove home from work to see why he was not answering his phone. What she found is out of my league; his lifeless body in their bedroom. The officer introduced me to her and her mother. I probed with questions, just to get her to talk it out. There is no possible way that she could go another moment with that inside her. Her emotions needed an outlet.

How do I approach a man sitting on the bedroom floor next to his deceased wife, crying as he holds her hand? "We cannot get him to move," the officer told me as I approached. That was his way of telling me that officials were on their way and needed to have clear access to the deceased. I had my work cut out for me. I took my place on the floor next to the husband, after asking his permission to do so. With my arm around him, I asked him to tell me what he could about what led up to this situation with his wife. "Have you and your wife shared a belief in God?"

Through tears, the answer was "yes."

"Would it be OK with you, if I say a prayer?"

He replied "yes." His sobbing overpowered my words. This was not the result of my training or pastoral expertise. It came directly from God. The words were His as well.

How do I talk with a traumatized boy, barely in his teen years, who was the only eyewitness to a homicide less than an hour before? The deceased lay in a driveway across from the boy's house. The boy and his dad witnessed the altercation as they sat on the porch and took cover inside. He was peeking through the blinds, when shots were fired. I received a detailed description of what he saw. He already had given details to several police officers. Each time he recalled a little more. I encourage him to talk freely to the officers, so they can help the family of his neighbor when they arrive. I am now listening to his fears. His question to me was "How can I feel safe?" Together we explore ways to feel safe and handle the vision he will carry in his mind for the rest of his life. Barely a teenager, he has just experienced something that few people will, regardless of how long they live.

Soon after officials arrive on the scene, news crews appear with their vans, antennae and cameras. Before the investigative work is very far along, networks have reported the event with as many pictures as they can gather. The report is aired, and doors are checked before retiring for the evening. Not much thought is given to the event after that.

The nightly news is enough to depress anyone. People make bad choices and those choices hurt others. It happened with the first brothers, Cain and Abel. Abel didn't deserve to be killed—especially by his own brother. However, Satan asserted his presence from the very beginning. He still does.

My Question

How did Adam and Eve deal with this? They didn't have access to Philippians 4:13 *"I can do all things through Christ who strengthens me."* Not only was it necessary to face the death of a son, their other son committed the murder—and fled.

We watch the news or read the reports, shrug and go about our lives happy that tragedy has not hit our families today.

"Praise be to the God and Father of our Lord Jesus Christ, the Father of compassion and the God of all comfort, who comforts us in all our troubles so that we can comfort those in any trouble with the comfort we ourselves receive from God." (2 Corinthians 4:3,4)

Dallas Willard describes it as the "striking availability of God to meet present human needs through our actions." My wife Brenda and I have been on the receiving end of "God's availability" through another person who was in the right place at the right time—not just once but often. We live with a consciousness of giving that back. Life's challenges are too hard to just "suck it up and take it like a man/woman." The God who created us *"knows our frame; He knows that we are dust."* (Psalms 103:14)

My Makeup Is Not My Own

I am the sum total of pieces of a number of good people. Jesus is at the top of my list of heroes. Jesus was the master at loving people. He loved good people, sinful people, downright evil people and hurting people. There is no more effective way I can model the behavior of my favorite hero, than to love everyone all the time.

God graciously placed several role models in my path. None of them did it right all the time—but Jesus did. I have thanked scores of people who have influenced me for good. Many of them gone from this life, but not without (to the best of my ability) me thanking them. Most of them are caught off guard. They never knew I was learning from them, until I told them. Colossians 3:15 tells us to "always be thankful." I thank everyone—including Jesus who constantly places me in situations where I can come one step closer to loving the way He did.

If you can possibly know my heart in these opening remarks, you will receive a glimpse of my heart's desire to return the comfort I have been given. It is my goal to communicate (through real experiences) the need for someone to be available to a hurting person. Trauma does not arrive at a convenient time. It cares not whether we are ready.

Chapter 2

Handling Trials—When It Hits Close to Home

A Vietnam veteran envisioned people in a circle putting
their challenges in that circle, to see if we could trade with someone.
Likely we would keep ours.

Not many would want to trade their woes for mine. When I am made aware of what goes on in the lives of others, it makes me prefer my own over theirs. Each heartache that I have endured has contributed to the person I am today. I'm not sure what "me" would look like, if I lived through the trials of someone else.

The untimely death of a loved one catches us off guard.

In 1973, on his 42nd birthday, my only brother was killed very early in the morning. It was a head-on collision that also took the life of the other driver. He was a veterinarian with a wife and two teenage daughters. Their oldest daughter was set to graduate high school in a few days. His physician, a personal friend, received the call, went to the house and knocked on the door, where the rest of the family was sleeping. We didn't receive the news for several hours. My heart has ached all these years for my sister-in-law and two nieces. That moment of trauma changed their lives from that point on. Mine too.

Questioning My Qualifications

When someone is facing a tremendous burden, I feel unqualified to help. A friend, who deals with people in trauma, tells me "if you ever feel confident going into a situation like that, it might be time to quit." I speak with the family of the victim, as they arrive on the scene. My heart connects with the mother. This is the woman who carried the child in her womb, gave birth and poured her life into his, as he grew. This is far from anything she wanted for his life. The older brother arrives, remembering all the times he protected him as they grew up. This time he wasn't there to help.

I met a man several years ago, who has become a dear friend. Soon after we met, he told me something that happened to him that still resonates with me. Family issues were impacting the children. He was called to the school of his young child. This child experienced an illness that needed medical attention. As they drove to the emergency room the child passed away—sitting next to dad.

Sitting with a widower, a gentleman younger than me outside of an assisted living center, his health issues have made it necessary to be a resident in this facility. He confided a phone call he got a few years back. It was to inform him that his son (in his 30's) was found hanging from a tree in the backyard of their home. My heart sank.

A gentleman driving home from work, was passing by the scene of an accident. The car loaded onto the wrecker belonged to his wife, yet she was nowhere around. Near the curb, he recognized a shoe that belonged to her. Thoughts raced through his mind. Police, fire, ambulance crews and even onlookers had left the scene and there was no one to ask. Finally, he located her and found her alive but seriously injured. Those few minutes of not knowing, were the most agonizing of his life. It was a powerful time of reflection. He recalled the last unkind word he had said to her, along with other acts of impatience, judgment, and thoughtlessness. He had plenty of time to regret them all and time to plan a path of healing.

I suppose there are those who will get through this life without much pain. Issues that consume them will be: 1. Is the lawn mowed? 2. Are the bills paid on time? 3. Will my car start when I turn the key? There are a host of things that require little strength or endurance. However, looks often are deceiving.

My sister-in-law is no longer dealing with my brother's death. She has been gone for many years. So have our parents. My brother's death was the only time I saw my dad show emotion of any kind, other than anger. As years passed, we adjusted; children were born, grandchildren were added and careers changed. That event was a catalyst that forced everyone to refocus. Many new things have eclipsed and overshadowed that single event, that brought so much pain years ago. It has been evidence that "life goes on." Survival is possible. Regardless of who we are or how long we stay here, no one's life is intended to be in vain. Every life has a purpose. It is when a bad choice (or no choice at all) is made that a person's destiny can be short changed

Chapter 3

Where is God?

"Consider it pure joy, my brothers and sisters, whenever
you face trials of many kinds, because you know that the testing of your
*faith produces perseverance." —*James 1: 2–3

If we are honest, trauma can shake us to the point of feeling abandoned by the God we have trusted in the past. In the midst of my own pain, I confess that I have a difficult time in worship. I sit there with my heart crushed and look around at fellow worshippers singing with far more euphoria than I can muster.

Not all the Psalms were written by David. Psalms 78 was written by Asaph. Asaph was a Levite in the court of King David, as well as a music leader and teacher. He spends 72 verses encouraging God's people with great details of how God protected and led his people. What struck me most, was the fact that Asaph was detailing events for which he was not an eyewitness. These events happened hundreds of years before his generation. Yet, he told about them in detail, in order to support his claim that God is reliable, aware, and works on behalf of His people. It is a constant theme throughout scripture. Asaph wanted his readers to recall the accounts of how God walked with His people. If He can do that for them, He also can do it for us. Count on it.

In our lives, we can look back and recall how God was in the middle of our own experiences. Brenda and I have been married for over fifty years. We have been through some very difficult times.

All our children have blessed us from the beginning. Our youngest child was a special blessing in demonstrating God's provisions. Four months after she was born, we were in the doctor's office for a regular visit. I pointed out something that I had shown Brenda. Her head was not symmetrical, and one eye socket was larger than the other. This was a shock to us. Our first two children grew up with no significant physical issues.

The primary doctor wanted to refer us to a neurologist, but the wait would be a few months. We were placed on a waiting list, having no idea what we were facing. I was discussing this with one of my good friends from graduate school. He said his wife's brother was a neurologist, "Let me see what I can do." He called me back the same day, with an appointment for us with his brother-in-law.

We did not even check our calendars. We just marked it down. That doctor determined that we needed a neurosurgeon. He was able to get us an appointment a few days later. An anticipated six-month wait turned into only a few days. Then came one of the most difficult things I have ever done. I carried our little four-month-old daughter toward the operating room of a hospital in Saint Paul, Minnesota, handed her to the anesthesiologist and sat outside the door of that room with Brenda, while a neurosurgeon operated on her for a Coronal Craniosynostosis.

We would have preferred dealing with colic or allergies. God saw us through this with a great deal of prayer and strength that we gained from one another. After the surgery, the surgeon emerged from the operating room and we could hear our daughter screaming. We were certain she wanted us. The surgeon anticipated, without us saying a word. Motioning his head toward the noise, he said, "That's normal. She is waking up. She did fine and will be fine." Maybe she was fine—but we were not.

I am in good company, when I read what David wrote in Psalms 13:

"O Lord, how long will you forget me? Forever?

How long will you look the other way?

How long must I struggle with anguish in my soul?

With sorrow in my heart every day?

How long will my enemy have the upper hand?

Turn and answer me, O Lord my God!

Restore the sparkle to my eyes, or I will die."

David questioned God's presence. Been there, done that.

David was confident of moving beyond his pain. *"But I trust in your unfailing love. I will rejoice because you have rescued me. I will sing to the Lord because He is good to me."* David had confidence: *"I will rejoice,"* I *will sing."* Somehow, David knew he would not feel abandoned for long. God had come through before and He will again. Been there, done that as well. However, this is not so easy, when the chips are down.

Listening to Others

Brenda shared with me a conversation she had with a stranger. We were at a loss as to why the lady chose to talk with Brenda, but she shared her story. Two months earlier, she had been driving her daughter to the doctor, when her daughter slumped over in the seat beside her. She called 911, an ambulance met her and the daughter was transported to the hospital. Her grandson was notified that his mother had been taken to the hospital. He got on his motorcycle to go to the hospital, had an accident and was killed. If James could place an arm around this lady, what would he say? James 1:2 is quite a challenge. "Consider it pure joy, my brothers and sisters, whenever you face trials of many kinds because you know that the testing of your faith produces perseverance." Joy? Really? Joy and trials just don't seem to fit together.

Brenda asked this dear lady how she found strength. Her daughter and grandson had died two hours apart. "God will get me through it."

Where do we find that confidence? What is our goal? An eternal perspective is essential. We are on our way to a better place. I grew up listening to my minister refer to this life as a "preparation place." Romans 8:21 promises "…Creation itself will be liberated from its bondage to decay and brought into the freedom and glory of the children of God."

Pain, loneliness, disappointment or the possibility of any kind of disappointment will be foreign to our environment there. This mother/grandmother expressed confidence in the promise from the Father: "Your daughter and grandson are with me." That's our goal anyway—right? Paul wrote, *"To be absent from the body is to be at home with the Lord."* (2 Corinthians 5:8) That is the comfort Brenda and I have used for almost thirty years, regarding our second grandchild. We have eight grandchildren—one already is "at home with the Lord."

This world is not home. Home is with the Lord. I, for one, need to focus more on the real goal.

It made no sense to Job that his life was disrupted the way it was. He (nor his children) had not done anything to deserve death. In fact, the book begins by declaring that "This man was blameless and upright; he feared God and shunned evil." (Job 1:1) When his children were taken, along with his significant possessions, his wife suggested that he "curse God and die." (Job 2:9) His immediate response was honorable: "Shall we accept good from God and not trouble?" (Verse 10)

I need confidence that God is here in the midst of my heart-wrenching pain. He feels it with me. However, he never apologizes for permitting me to endure it. He didn't do it to Job and I don't expect his apology either.

Chapter 4

Credibility

"This High Priest of ours understands our weaknesses, for he faced all the same testing we do, yet he did not sin." —Hebrews 4:15

"Easy for YOU to say. You're not feeling what I'm feeling." Isn't that our sentiment when someone offers a trite word of comfort in the midst of our pain? There are certain things that we just don't learn in a counseling course. Limited comfort will come in a counselor's office. It's always the case that the trauma I am attempting to comfort is not mine, unless I experience it myself.

Jesus provides ultimate credibility. Hebrews 4:16 encourages us to "Come boldly to the throne of our gracious God. There we will receive his mercy, and we will find grace to help us when we need it most."

Still difficult? Amen to that. However, at least we can't complain about having no one to talk with, who really can identify with our hurt.

A frequent one-liner in scripture is "fear not." Those are nice words, but I can't say I have spent my life avoiding fear. I even fear fear itself. That was a significant warning by Franklin D. Roosevelt at his first inauguration. I am not sure I ever understood it. However, then I read the book of Job. Job was one of those men who had everything going for him but quickly lost it all. In Job 3:25,26 Job declared, "What I feared has come upon me." By this statement, Job admitted fear of being separated from all the good things with which he had been blessed (i.e. his children and his possessions). They were all taken from him in a short time. No wonder it took over 40 chapters in the Bible to tell his story.

As I spend time "counting my blessings" and then "what if" all the scenarios, I begin to fear fear. Brenda is better at this than me. She is the one dealing with a form of cancer. I am certain that I have fretted over the situation far more than she has. She reminds me that we must get the most out of each day. I need to hear that. I know the Bible says it, but it is a different story when a person is actually faced with it. It is easy to declare this from a position of comfort.

In *The Horse and His Boy,* The lion spared Aravis. She speaks to the Hermit: "I say! I have had luck." The Hermit replies: "Daughter, I have now lived a hundred and nine winters in this world and have never yet met any such thing as Luck."

My hero doctor has a building named after him. That came at a great price, because he persisted in something he believed in, even through difficult circumstances.

What a boost to our pride and ego for a building to be named after us. It would give us some assurance that we made a recognizable contribution and added value to others. However, rather than BE him, I'm glad I KNEW him. I don't know how well I would have handled all the challenges he faced. This amazing man lived into his nineties and was so filled with humility, I am certain he never (before he left) understood the full impact of the work he had done. Future generations will receive a chance, that they may not have had otherwise. Brenda is one of them.

Moses did a great deal in leading the Israelites out of Egypt, through forty years in the desert and to the brink of the Promised Land. He did all this work, only to be told that he would not experience it himself. God took him to a high place to see it from a distance. His life on the earth ended at age 120, without him experiencing the result of all the work he did. He continued to receive credit throughout scripture, even though he was not around to hear.

In Fort Worth, a hospital bears the name of Ben Hogan on the building where I have had surgery. Mr. Hogan's legacy was no accident. He made a name for himself in golf, before the days of high dollar tournament winnings. He endured tragedy in his life. At a very young age, his father took his own life. He had a serious automobile accident that almost claimed his life. His recovery was slow, but he recovered and played golf again. He and his wife lived well but had no children. Much money for good causes has been raised through the years after his death, thanks to his name associated with them. This was all done after his death, so he saw none of it.

I will be satisfied having my name printed on the hearts of those who loved me in this life. I cannot think of a better legacy.

Where Do My Fears Go?

As I write this, I am facing a medical procedure called a cardioversion. It entails taking blood thinners and monitoring the density of the blood. An electric charge will then be sent through my heart to address the atrial fibrillation. I have been discussing this with a doctor I met at the gym, who is following my progress. I shared my lack of 100% confidence. I told him what the people in the cardiology area said to help calm my fears: "We do this every day." He said, *"Yes, but it's not their heart."* Wow! Did that hit home. I am now less fearful than in the beginning. I can also offer words of compassion and assurance to someone facing a similar procedure, with trust that I am offering something appropriate.

Like many, I've experienced ultimate examples of credibility. Our oldest daughter Holly was at our home with her children. Her two-month-old son was sleeping in a crib that we kept there. When she made a routine check on the child, she found him cold, blue in color and unresponsive. She began CPR, emergency calls were made, and care flight transported the child. The family piled in the car and raced to the children's hospital. The baby did not survive.

The funeral home was packed with friends and family offering support. Holly and I were on our knees looking at the remains of this beautiful boy, wondering how to trust a God whose view of life and death was different from our own. A lady from church walked up behind us with a photo album in her hand. She asked, "Can I share some photos of my baby who died?" The entire situation changed from that point on. No Bible quotes. No feeble attempts at encouraging words. Just someone reaching out with their heart. Who could question this lady's credibility?

My wife was going through brutal chemotherapy. I searched for some helpful reading, so I could be an effective caretaker to her. Lessons came from others that I would not have learned on my own. She needed me to be fully present. I found myself resting my hand on her back during the night, following every breath for assurance of life.

I learned, through this experience, to choose my words wisely. I now avoid comments, such as "everything is going to be fine." That is a direct quote from one article. No one needs false comfort. I certainly don't want to offer something I can't deliver.

Listening with Compassion and Commonality

Yesterday, I spent a lot of time with a lifelong friend. Kenny is as close as a brother could be. After a twenty-year break from cancer, it has returned. Inserting a port turned out to be a terrible experience for him. It placed him in intensive care for the night. He knows what I have been through with Brenda. He also knows how much I love him.

There are moments like this, when I feel the most inadequate. I bent over and put my hand on a woman's shoulder. Minutes before I arrived, she had been told by the hospital personnel that her son did not survive the gunshot. How can I say anything of value? I've not experienced a situation like this. I can't relate first hand. I was warned she had been disrespectful to the hospital chaplains, who had attempted to console her. This was just one of many times I have directly asked God to take over. He has had the experience of having his son's life taken. I don't even recall what I said, but I do recall her reaching up, holding my hand and saying "Thank you. Thank you for coming."

Our Sorrows Are Nothing New

David was described as a man after God's heart. (1 Samuel 13:14) Yet David was just as subject to making bad choices as anyone. Nathan the prophet confronted him with a big one with four words: "You are that man," (2 Samuel 12:7) As a result, David wrote one of his most moving psalms (51) I had a wonderful college professor who gave me credit for his entire course simply because I wrote out that psalm from memory. It still chokes me up to read it. David had a way of returning to God, when he stumbled and needed comfort. He knew it was safe there.

The account of David's son Amnon violating his half-sister Tamar is a captivating story of a parent caught in the middle. It is recorded in 2 Samuel 13. David was the father of both. This was a situation with no closure. Tamar was violated by her half-brother, changing the family dynamic forever. With good intentions, David directed Tamar to go to her brother to help. Without knowing it, David assisted Amnon in carrying out his evil plan. "When King David heard all this, he was furious." (Verse 21)

He had committed an indiscretion with Bathsheba, yet was unable to instill good judgment in his own children. One of my favorite Psalms is 108:13. David places the victory where it belongs. It is not my ability to "suck it up" or "be strong." David asks God "Give us aid against the enemy, for human help is worthless." He then expresses confidence in God's role, "With God we will gain the victory, and he will trample down our enemies."

A great deal of the self-destructive behavior dealt with by law enforcement, is the feeling of failure by an individual to carry out his expectations in life (i.e. be a good provider for his family, direct his children into responsible behavior, control his own propensity to addiction, etc.). We take too much on ourselves. It is admittedly a challenge to trust God to "trample down our enemies."

Absolom, (David's other son) waited patiently for two years to find an opportunity to kill his half-brother Amnon for what he did. When Jonadab announced to David that Amnon had been killed, "the king's sons came in, wailing loudly. The king, too, and all his attendants wept very bitterly." One might think David would rejoice over the death of Amnon for the evil he had done to his sister. Not so. He was angry over his behavior but grieved over his death.

Sometimes I wonder why God doesn't save extreme situations for those who do not walk with Him. Let the bad people suffer and leave the good folks alone. No wonder David questioned God's presence in Psalms 13.

It's easy to think we are the only ones troubled when unwelcomed events strike. Been there, done that. Psalms 73:7 expresses the mentality that everyone (even the unruly) has it made with ease and success—except us. Hebrews 4:15 offers us assurance that (through Jesus) our Heavenly Father faced all the same testing as we do. He created His son as well as those who mistreated Jesus and put Him to death. It is stunning to contemplate the heart of a Father of whom Jesus said, "My God, my God, why have you forsaken me?" Could God have intervened and prevented His son from suffering? Of course, He could have. He witnessed the persecution of the Hebrew nation by their enemies, even turning away from them and allowing them to suffer the consequences of their choices. History would have been re-written had He intervened.

David was not the only one who suffered when his enemies brought him to his knees. The Father witnessed the beheading of John the Baptizer. We read the account but hardly can imagine the details. God saw every move of the ax and severing of this man's head from his body. He was present at the stoning of Stephen and He was in the middle of the terrible suffering by the Apostle Paul, described in 2 Corinthians 4.

In order to take one more ride, it is necessary that we trust his presence in our lives.

Chapter 5

The Risk of Relationships

*"The Lord is close to the brokenhearted; He rescues those
whose spirits are crushed."* —Psalms 34:18

How could we avoid the risk of relational pain? Imagine yourself alone. The apostle Paul in 1 Corinthians 7:7, 8 confessed that it would be fine to be single, like he chose to be. Jesus chose the single life for himself. However, if we choose to marry, we run the risk of being separated from our spouse by death—and it happens every day. If we choose to have children, we take that same risk—this, too happens every day. "No one can live forever, all will die. No one can escape the power of the grave." Psalms 89:48. So, what are the choices?

Our grandson did not live three full months on this earth. Nevertheless, years after he has been gone, we recall the joy we experienced in that short time. He smiled at me first. We named him after his grandmother. He was the second grandchild and fostered mothering instincts in his big sister. She is now the mother to three boys—and an incredible one at that. We think of Brendan Tyler every day and it happened in 1990. Would it have been better had he not come? We don't think so.

I read about a 21-year-old girl who passed away unexpectedly. The girl's father said, "If God had told us when this child was born, 'You can have her, but you can only have her for 21 years, I would have accepted." Those years brought unspeakable joy in the lives of these parents and there was no other way to experience that joy than to accept the risk.

I recently addressed this with the mother of a 24-year-old girl whose life was taken by cancer. She could not imagine her life without her daughter in it—even for a short time. Even though she is hurt by the separation, she would not trade the past twenty-four years with this precious child.

In the midst of his despair, Job cursed the day of his birth. That was God's business. The best we can do is go with it.

These Lessons Are Not Easily Learned

Paul's life was not a party. He suffered untold pain and persecution. Prior to his road to Damascus experience, he lived life with the upper hand. He had status in the Jewish faith and was in the majority at the stoning of Stephen. It wasn't until he "changed sides" that he began to suffer the things he previously had dealt to others. He had learned to be content with a life of suffering (Philippians 4:12)

We miss a great deal, when we go straight to verse 13. It always has intrigued me that he used the word "learned." It was not something that came naturally for Paul. Nor will it for us. It must be learned. Paul fully understood that what he was seeking would not be fully realized in this life. It is in Philippians 3:12–14 that he describes his effort to press on toward the life that really matters.

Chris Kyle was a Navy Seal sniper. He served four tours in the Iraq War and was awarded several commendations for heroism and service in combat. He and a friend were killed at a gun range in 2013. A movie "American Sniper" was made based on Chris's book of the same name.

Taya Kyle, his widow, related her fear in a Fort Worth Star-Telegram article. She said she was scared of being left alone with two young children— "Scared that if I went to the darkest place I really felt I would not come out of it, and I had to work through that and find the courage in time, to find places in times where I could let it out, or it would just live there simmering under the surface forever and have me constantly on the verge of a breakdown. And if I'm super, super honest about why I think I'm OK, it's because I believe Chris is still with me. And if I really didn't think I'd ever see him again, I wouldn't make it."

She then makes a profound admission: "I'd be a fool to not live this life and see the blessings for what they are and see the beautiful people in this world who are stronger than I am and who do more things than I do and try to give back."

Extreme Emotional Pain

It would be rare to get through this life without it. We have no choice which events come our way. We have no choice, as to how or when a loved one is taken. We might think it would be more acceptable to deal with a natural death than one that is accidental and unexpected.

A gentleman described years of being at his wife's side, who was suffering from a terminal illness. When she passed, he dealt with the necessary things, then went hunting in several states. He explained that his grieving had been accomplished. His wife's death was no surprise.

Contrast that with a sudden loss. With a police officer, I was called to the scene of a suicide. The man, in his early 40's, became so distraught over a troubled relationship, that he took his own life. His parents were deceased and the relationship with his siblings had deteriorated long ago. Only an aunt and her daughter were close—and this was a step-aunt.

Psalms 34:18 was a passage familiar to both and we spent some time discussing its relevance to the situation: *"The Lord is close to the brokenhearted; He rescues those whose spirits are crushed."*

Gary Thomas wrote, "Read through the entire Bible, and I promise you, you won't find one reference to a 'crown in heaven' that goes to the person who had the 'happiest' life on earth. That reward just doesn't exist. Nor is there a heavenly ribbon for the Christian who felt the least amount of pain."

Kahili Gibran put it this way: "It is by the depth of our sorrows that we know our joys."

Orson Wells said, "In Italy, for 30 years under the Borgias, they had warfare, terror, murder and bloodshed, but they produced Michelangelo, Leonardo da Vinci and the Renaissance. In Switzerland, they had brotherly love, 500 years of democracy and peace and what did they produce? The cuckoo clock."

Philip Yancy wrote: "God neither protects Christians with a shield of health nor provides a quick, dependable solution to all suffering. Christians populate hospital wards, asylums and hospices in approximate proportion to the world at large."

The God who made us, certainly anticipated these off-the-chart times in our lives. The scriptures are full of such promises. In addition, what He has provided must be the correct remedy. After all, He made us and knows our needs.

Chapter 6

Do Things Really Happen for a Reason?

*"The Lord is not slow in keeping his promise, as some
understand slowness. Instead he is patient with you, not wanting
anyone to perish, but everyone to come to repentance."* —2 Peter 3:9

I am a student of the Bible. It is my commitment that this book is completely" inspired by God and written for our learning." (2 Timothy 3:16) It serves as an "owner's manual" from the creator to those He created. It is an obligation to keep scripture in context. When Moses declared that "the Lord will protect you from all sickness. He will not let you suffer from the terrible diseases you knew in Egypt," this promise was not made to me (I wish).

Paul wrote to the Thessalonians to "mind your own business and work with your hands." (1 Thessalonians 4:11) Would it be sinful for a person to choose a career as an accountant, lawyer, bank president or some profession, where the mind would be the primary tool?

It wasn't long ago that our preacher dealt with a series of passages taken out of context. It is sad that we spend any of our time applying meaning to passages that is not there. I need real hope—not false hope. My childhood mind reveled in the stories Mother read to me that ended with "and they lived happily ever after." She avoided my question each time: "but what happened after this?" "Happily, ever after" sounds nice but not realistic.

One of the lessons that sparked a significant amount of response was this: "God will not give us any more than we can handle." For years, I qualified that by wording it this way: "God will not give us any more than He knows we can handle." I am still adjusting to the fact that one of my convictions has taken a beating. The passage is found in 1 Corinthians 10:13:" No temptation has overtaken you except what is common to mankind. And God is faithful: he will not let you be tempted beyond what you can bear. But when you are tempted, he will also provide a way out so that you can endure it."

This passage deals with temptation and that is Satan's job. Joseph ran from Potiphar's wife, when temptation faced him. Job refused the advice of his wife to "curse God and die." Jesus resisted Satan, by making the proper application of scripture in response to the enemy's incorrect use of those passages.

One of the favorite passages our son and I shared when he was a child was James 4:7 "Resist the devil and he will flee (this was said with force) from you. Come close to God and He will come close to you." Even a growing boy could understand who takes the initiative in our response both to God and Satan. We take the first step. Jesus is our "weapon" against Satan and He "stands at the door and knocks" (Revelation 3:20)

We could continue to list passages that are applied incorrectly or taken out of context. Raphael McManus stated it this way: "Are you willing to live a life that honors God and reflects His character and leaves the outcome to Him?" Either He is trustworthy, or he is not. I believe He is.

Pain hurts, and it hurts for a long time. Have you ever had the news given to you that someone you love has died? I have—at least three times. I have visited several times with a former colleague. Both of us had one brother. Both of our brothers died suddenly in auto accidents. Each time we recall our stories to one another, I am struck by the detail we both bring and how much compassion I feel, when he relates his experience. I know because I feel it too. Why are we reliving those experiences 45–50 years after they happened? It doesn't consume either of us, but those experiences went into shaping us into the person that we are today.

I recall Brenda calling and telling me I need to come home. The memory is in slow motion. Her words and my heart floated in space, as she said, "Your dad called. Bob was killed last night in a car wreck." As I struggled to get my breath, Brenda put a family friend on the phone. She simply sat silently on the phone for five or ten minutes, while I cried. A few years earlier, this kind woman had found her husband deceased outside, where he had been washing the car. She shared that experience with me many times.

My friend does the same thing with the memory of his brother's death. He can describe in detail the reaction of his mother and friends, as well as his own. I know he understands my story and I understand his.

It is amazing how it works. A memorable police call, was to a home of grandparents who were raising their grandchildren. One was lying in bed (in the grandparent's room) deceased. The grandmother was not able to sit still, even for one second. Her husband was confident that this would lead his wife to a "nervous breakdown." The family made it through and, the grandmother admitted to me that the most helpful thing she heard from me was about the passing of my own grandchild. Somehow, that knowledge brought comfort to her and gave credibility to the situation.

Paul wrote, "Are they Hebrews? So am I. Are they Israelites? So am I. Are they Abraham's descendants? So am I. (2 Corinthians 11:22) It was those things Paul had in common with others, that allowed him to "become all things to all men." (1 Corinthians 9:22)

I heard it again today: "everything that has happened to me has happened for a reason." It certainly sounds nice, but I do not find it in the Bible. I take full responsibility for my poor behavior and am not willing to factor it in as part of the script for my life.

It also is a struggle for me to consider how much God knows about the world and wonder if He might choose to eliminate some things from His knowledge. We are quick to say that God can do anything, but I beg to differ. He can only do things that are consistent with His will and purpose. *"He cannot be tempted by evil,"* (Malachi 3:6) *"He cannot lie,"* (Titus 1:2) Can He make a square with three sides or a triangle with four sides? Can He make a pancake that is flat only on one side?

When Abraham drew back his hand to run a knife through Isaac, God stopped him and said, "Now I know that you fear God, because you have not withheld from me your son, your only son" (Genesis 22:12) The word for "know" in the original language carries the meaning of "fully know." Did God not know how Abraham would respond to the command to sacrifice his son? Of course, He did.

It is difficult to accept that our lives are so scripted, that there is a reason for everything that happens to us. Someone would have to explain why our grandson came and left in less than three months. No one has sufficiently explained why some homes are spared in a wildfire and some are not. There is no adequate explanation of why some people survive a mass shooting and others do not. We are simply faced with the task of getting through events like Columbine, Las Vegas and other difficult and unexpected tragedies as best we can and placing them into the history of our minds.

I do find that we are creatures with free will and that was a big risk on God's part. He knew that we would need a savior and began planning from the beginning.

I Don't Know

Now, I am willing to cave a little. Perhaps there IS a purpose for everything that happens to us. Perhaps God DOES NOT allow us to go through anything HE KNOWS we cannot handle. After all—He is our creator.

Certainly, God had a plan for Joseph. He came from being the red-headed step brother to slavery to the number two person in Egypt. Four hundred and thirty years later, we see a strong nation (under the leadership of Joshua) conquering the land that God committed to His people long before.

Do we have a patient God or what? Peter thought so: "With the Lord a day is like a thousand years, and a thousand years are like a day. The Lord is not slow in keeping his promise, as some understand slowness. Instead, he is patient with you, not wanting anyone to perish, but everyone to come to repentance." (2 Peter 3:9)

Grief can hold us captive, or we can move forward and become a better person. In the heat of grief, it is next to impossible (with our finite minds) to see any purpose at all. We may never see it during our life. We need to read a lot of history to put the pieces together. In the midst of grief, I am not going to say to anyone that there is a purpose. My safest and most logical response to the question "why me?" is simply "I DON'T KNOW."

Do we know that God can make something good come out of a tragedy? YOU BET WE DO. A couple does marriage counseling individually and together. The husband's first wife suffered through years of a horrible illness, then went to heaven. He speaks her praises to their audience. The current wife then speaks up and tells how much she looks forward to meeting her predecessor. So much of what her husband is today, came from her godly influence. I must say Amen to that.

God put Brenda in my life. It was a match that refocused me into a man after His heart. It's been a long, difficult journey of bumps and bruises. However, the outcome has humbled me. If you had known us when we met, you would have seen two very opposite people. The result has been astounding. I am willing to give God credit for that.

Another Dilemma

I'm going to make a statement, but you have no way of knowing its validity. **When I am facing someone who has experienced tragedy, I want compassion to be genuine.**

I have been on the receiving end of compassion. We can fake many things but we cannot fake compassion.

The police take me into situations, where true compassion is essential. Occasionally, compassion needs to be poured out to the officer. Many of the challenges Brenda and I have endured, have better prepared us for those times when we stand face to face with someone who is experiencing "off the charts" pain. That never is the time to be fake.

In the book of Job, we receive insight into the spiritual world. Job did not have this preview when his world fell apart. "One day the angels came to present themselves before the Lord, and Satan also came with them. The Lord said to Satan, 'Where have you come from?'

Satan answered the lord, 'From roaming throughout the earth, going back and forth on it.'

Then the Lord said to Satan, 'Have you considered my servant Job? There is no one on earth like him; He is blameless and upright, a man who fears God and shuns evil.'

'Does Job fear God for nothing?' Satan replied.

'Have you not put a hedge around him and his household and everything he has? You have blessed the work of his hands, so that his flocks and herds are spread throughout the land. But stretch out your hand and strike everything he has, and he will surely curse you to your face.'

The Lord said to Satan, 'Very well, then, everything he has is in your power, but on the man, himself do not lay a finger.'"

"Then Satan went out from the presence of the Lord."

It was at this point that the bottom dropped out of Job's life. However, he had no knowledge of the meeting between God and Satan. Isn't it interesting how God spoke up for Job and Satan sought to discredit him? We enter each challenge unaware of the events going on in God's spiritual world. God trusted Job's character and dared Satan to discredit him. It might have worked but Job was grounded from the beginning: "At this, Job got up and tore his robe and shaved his head. Then he fell to the ground in worship and said: 'Naked I came from my mother's womb and naked I will depart. The Lord gave, and the Lord has taken away; May the name of the Lord be praised.' In all this, Job did not sin by charging God with wrongdoing." (Job 1:20–22)

This statement indicates where Job stood. It is not a statement by a man with super powers to withstand anything that came his way. Several chapters are devoted to the feeble efforts of his friends to explain everything. Job went off into questioning God's actions and even demanding an explanation for what was happening. In the end, Job reverted to his real character and responded with the same confidence God had in him. God is able to take that kind of response from us. I sure am glad. It is a true picture of His love and patience toward us.

Tim Madigan is a freelance writer in Fort Worth. On the day after the death of Fred Rogers (February 27, 2003), Tim wrote an article recalling important details of his friendship with this good man. Our oldest daughter was a devoted fan of Mr. Rogers' Neighborhood as a child. We overheard (and sometimes watched with her) those episodes and sang along with her.

Madigan's article was reprinted in the *Fort Worth Star-Telegram* on October 25, 2017. During their friendship, Fred walked Tim through some struggles with his demons (Fred referred to them as Furries). In a conversation mentioning cancer being experienced by one of Fred's friends, he said "I am angry at cancer," pounding harder on the piano keys.

Fred said, "With grief there is, inevitably, some times of anger, and you know, God can take our anger." Then he paused and said "You're ministering to me, Tim. By listening, you minister to me." Listening gives me comfort in God's calling. Often it is the best option at a tragic moment.

I recall the ten minutes of silence on the phone with our family friend, as I learned of my brother's death. She did not speak, until I did. She need not give advice on how to accept the news of my brother's death. Listening to my crying was enough. She cried as well. I knew her story and had no doubts about her qualification to be on the phone with me at that time. She was immediately elevated to hero status for being there for us. That took courage. It also coincided with the heart God had given her through her own experiences.

In 1998, Fred Rogers was featured in a cover story of *Esquire Magazine*. It was a special issue on "New American Heroes" and Fred Rogers was chosen.

Junod wrote of the time Mister Rogers visited a boy with cerebral palsy, who was so angry about his condition that he wanted to die. However, during their visit, Mister Rogers had a favor to ask: "Will you pray for me?" Fred said. The boy was dumfounded. All his life, people had been praying for him. Why would this famous man turn the tables? However, Mister Rogers did. From that day forward, the boy kept Mister Rogers in his prayers, and he no longer talked about wanting to die."

Junod commended Mr. Rogers for his use of reverse psychology "aimed to distract the boy from his suffering." "Oh, heavens no, Tom!" Fred told Junod. "I didn't ask for his prayers for him. I asked for me. I asked because I think that anyone who has gone through challenges like that, must be very close to God. I asked him because I wanted his intercession."

I heard the directive. "We are not people with a solution. We are the presence of God." I accept that assignment. In the event words are appropriate, I will train every way possible to make certain the words are proper and relevant.

Chapter 7

Choices Are for Life

"The only really unethical thing for you to do is for you not to take responsibility for your decisions." —John Paul Sartre

The choices we make each day bear consequences for life. We live in a society that looks for someone to blame. McDonald's is sued because a customer spilled hot coffee in their own lap. One group of people oppress another. I have said and done things to hurt others.

Who hasn't? I have been hurt by others, as well. I have spent much of my life apologizing, asking forgiveness and making amends. It is up to the offended person and me to bury the hatchet, see how we can capitalize on that experience and go forward in the most constructive way. I looked to other men who had lived more responsibly and made better choices than the man who fathered me.

Something someone said to me years ago, still resonates. Mrs. Hunter, one of my high school English teachers said, "You are a very capable young man." At that point in my life, no one else was communicating such value to me. I have a copy of a letter I wrote to Mrs. Hunter, long after I had married. I assured her that the encouraging words she chose to speak to me had a long-term effect. It crushed me to hear back from her telling me that (after all the years she spent as a school teacher) my letter was the first to thank her. I still recall her clasping her fingers together and putting them under her chin, as she talked about Mark Twain. It is as clear as yesterday, when she told of meeting Robert Frost and being kissed on the forehead by this literary genius. Those stories influenced me to take the writing of these men into the rest of my life.

Our heroes will not know they are our heroes, if we don't tell them. I think about Mrs. Hunter's words of confidence in me when I am in a police car, transporting a prisoner to jail and listening to him blame everyone but himself. I love to say to them "You are a better person than this. I will pray that you will use this experience to refocus your life in a way to make everyone who loves you proud."

Moving On

The Prime Minister of Japan came to Pearl Harbor 75 years after the Japanese attack that launched the U.S. into WWII. He had been to the Punch Bowl cemetery and paid his respects. Later in the day, he met our President at the Arizona Memorial. His government had stated that their prime minister did not intend to apologize for the attack on December 7, 1941 (the day I was born). Should that concern us? If he did apologize, what would that accomplish?

I was sent to Japan to serve in the military at age 18, 15 years after the Japanese surrender. I found the citizens of that country to be very contrite, humble, and respectful. They did not consider me an intruder in any way. I knew that the people I was meeting, had nothing to do with what happened at Pearl Harbor.

The same is true for other injustices throughout history. My heart is burdened by those who sense a feeling of subordination because of their ethnicity. However, we don't need anyone blaming someone else for their bad choices and lot in life.

The Personal Tragedy

We all have made bad choices that have a lasting effect. Consider the act of suicide. Someone told me how his father's choice to end his life still affects him over thirty years later. His children asked him how old his father was, when he died. "In his 40's." It was followed by the question: "How did he die?" It was difficult to tell his children (and others who ask) that his father made the decision to end his own life. His father's choice had a lifetime consequence.

Suicide has been called "the ultimate act of selfishness" or "a permanent solution for a temporary problem." It is reported that 38,000 people in the U.S. take their own lives each year. Reports indicate that 64% of all suicides are a surprise to the family. There are many situations that drive a person to this level of despair. These instances increase at the end of the year, during the holidays. Many families and survivors are affected by this single act on behalf of the deceased loved one.

This is a choice with a generational effect. If a person takes his own life, his children are four to five times more likely to make the same choice for themselves. I recently learned that more lives of first responders are ended in this way each year, than in the line of duty.

Anyone who has been with someone they love when they draw their last breath, can detail that experience throughout the remainder of their lives often. I am called on to conduct a funeral for someone I never knew personally. These families may have no church connection, have been inactive for some time, or their own minister is not available. They are seeking closure on the life of someone they love. Prior to the service, I visit with the closest family members, asking questions that help me assemble thoughts that will celebrate the life of that person. When I ask, "Can you describe for me your last moments with your mom?" the responses I receive are emotional for both of us. Then I ask, "Months and years from now, when you see a picture of your mom, what thoughts will you have?" It is another emotional moment.

The choice to make the last moments meaningful, will have lasting value. I have a dear friend whose oldest daughter endured a long illness, that eventually took her into eternity. As she was approaching the end of this life, she did something amazing. She called each child in the family to her. Then she spoke directly to each of them with words of hope and confidence. My guess is that these kids will remember that experience throughout their lives.

Chapter 8

Negative Memories

"Oh, the joys of those who do not follow the advice of the wicked, or stand around with sinners, or join in with mockers." —Psalms 1:1

I was raised in a home where value was not communicated, and frustration often was expressed through rage. I struggled with these experiences my entire life. It took me well over five years of marriage, before I could utter the words "I love you." They were not words spoken in my childhood home.

It was a fellow ministerial student, who repeated them to me each day of our training. Coming from one man to another, gave it enormous impact. One day I ventured out and said it back. To my astonishment, my world did not crumble, and all of my preconceived ideas vanished. That began a new chapter in my life. My heart responded and gave me tools to work with and improve my behavior.

My dad was an alcoholic. To this day, I bear scars from my home life. I am afraid my own children have picked up some of these. They know I don't live as a victim and I don't want that for them. I have spent a lot of time apologizing. It was my decision to NOT follow in the steps of my own father. I looked to other men who lived more responsibly and made better choices than the man who fathered me.

Jess Lair wrote: "Each of our behaviors has certain immediate and inflexible consequences. Damage is done, and we may spend the rest of our life making amends."

Dad was not all bad. I have met people who worked with him. Many of them gave rave reviews of his work ethic and creativity. Dad worked as a tool designer at an aircraft plant. I've heard accounts of how he stunned his coworkers, by designing a tool to work on these flying machines.

I also witnessed his heart in action. It was in 1949. A torrential rain in Fort Worth displaced many families. Dad took me along to rescue families from their flooded homes. He invited a family to stay with us, until they could arrange lodging. Five kids slept in the same bed—three from this family plus my younger sister and me. That remains an example to me of "hands-on" help for someone in need.

I'm Not Exempt from Fault

As a young husband, there are some painful memories of things I did that I still regret. Our oldest daughter came along a month after our first anniversary. We were in college, living in an apartment near the campus. The apartment complex had a swimming pool and we spent hot summer days there. I wanted to make a swimmer out of Holly and had seen accounts of how it worked for others. Some people just put their toddlers in the water and they would swim naturally. It didn't work for me. I took her under the water with me and came up laughing. I thought she was laughing along with me, but she was choking and terrified. As a result, this grandmother will not put her face under water in a pool today. I regret my misguided effort.

They had side-by-side parking at the apartment complex. Next to where I usually parked, a neighbor would park her car so far to the right, that it crowded out my favorite space. One frustrating day, I opened my door to exit. It would not open enough for me to get out. Out of anger, I moved my car to another location, but not before smashing my door into the car next to me. This left a sizable scratch on the side of the neighbor's car and even a larger mark on my heart for years. A short while later, we bought a mobile home and moved away. I went by the apartment several times to confess, apologize and offer to pay for repairs. I never connected with our former neighbor. I have carried that regret with me for many years and have learned new ways to handle frustration.

My first pulpit preaching job was at a small church in northern Mississippi. I served there for two and a half years, while completing a master's degree. Our son had been born, just before moving. One Sunday morning during my sermon, Brenda worked to get him quiet. He was really bellowing like he was hurting—little did I know that he was. After a few minutes of this disruption, I paused long enough to say, "Please take him out." She did. I have regretted doing this for over 40 years and will continue to do so, even though I know I cannot reverse what happened. As it turned out, Paul had a continual ear infection that not only caused pain and discomfort but also impeded his growth and development. It took a specialist in Memphis to detect it. Once it was healed, he was a much calmer child.

When my mother was in her 80s, it was a burden for her to get out of her chair and move around the room. I went by her apartment almost every day to check on her. One day we had a disagreement (Mother could be critical at times). I got up and walked out of the room, without saying a word. As I was walking out, she was apologizing, crying and pleading, "Please don't leave." I have carried that image in my mind for years. Mother left this world at peace with her children and grandchildren. Thankfully, I was holding her hand and repeating the words "I love you, Mother."

Where's the Delete Button?

I always have wondered how the apostle Paul dealt with his regrets. That question came to mind, as I stood over the spot in Rome that is claimed to be the resting place of his earthly remains. After his conversion, others certainly remembered his background. He was able to say, "I have fulfilled my duty to God in all good conscience to this day." (Acts 23:1) Although he killed followers of God, he did it in good conscience. Often in his writing, he expresses gratitude for the grace of God. He referred to himself as "the worst of sinners." (1 Timothy 1:15)

On my computer keyboard, I have a "delete" button. I don't have one of those for my life. As our children were growing up, we taught them the importance of the words we speak. Once I speak hurtful words, I can't take them back—words only go in one direction. Although forgiveness is assured, damage can linger for a lifetime.

As I work with the police, much of what I see crushes my heart. This has expanded my perspective on life. Several police officers have told me that crime and misbehavior are focused on about two percent of the population. Ninety-eight percent are fine and upstanding. However, Satan introduced evil into the world early in human history.

Recently I saw a t-shirt on a woman that said, "It is what it is." I have attempted for years to change "what it is," but to no avail. Scripture offers some strong admonitions about the kind of people we spend our time with. "Bad company corrupts good morals" (1 Cor. 15:33), "Stay away from fools, for you won't find knowledge on their lips." (Proverbs 14:7), "Oh, the joys of those who do not follow the advice of the wicked, or stand around with sinners, or join in with mockers." (Psalms 1:1) This is a verse our oldest daughter and I repeated together each night at bedtime. She has it committed to memory today.

Toward the end of a shift with a veteran police officer, we finally had time to stop and eat. I will always remember the conversation we shared over our meal. His mother was fifteen, when he was born. Her parents didn't think she was equipped to raise a son, so they took that responsibility. His father married his mother and the officer developed a close relationship with all four adults. When his mother was diagnosed with a terminal illness, his dad had a conversation with him about accepting the inevitable. He said, "There is not a thing I can do to change things, so I just have to accept it, learn from it and go on."

We heard that same thing last week in our small Bible study group. Our facilitator and his wife have been dealing with her cancer for some time. She took a few days to spend Grandparents' Day with their grandchildren a few states away. It was the first time they had been separated, since all this began. I shared his tears, when he told our group that he has come face to face with the fact that there is nothing he can do to change what is. All he can do is be grateful for the good days, learn from it and go forward. The t-shirt has some merit. It really "is what it is."

Chapter 9

Peripheral Damage

"For whoever finds me finds life and receives favor from the lord.
But those who miss me injure themselves." —Proverbs 8:35

As I write this, Brenda and I are experiencing one of the worse times of our marriage. It does not involve our choices, rather the choices of someone we love a great deal. We invested years of effort into all our children and grandchildren. It always is painful to observe choices made, that are contrary to the prayerful guidance we provided. Perhaps to some degree, it DOES have to do with our own choices. We made the choice to have each of our children (no accidents or surprises). The choice to have them, along with the timing, was carefully planned. Our love for them, and the grandchildren that would follow, was worth the risk of any disappointments. The verse in Proverbs makes it clear that there is the risk that others are injured as well. That is the peripheral damage.

Together, we have conveyed love to every offspring in this family. When we part company, our grandchildren are quicker with the words "I love you" than we are. However, we are still faced with carrying some hurts throughout our lives. Our imperfections haven't diminished God's love for us. (Roman 8:31–30) Neither has disappointments detracted our love from those who are a product of this marriage.

Family tension is not a new concept. Isaac and Rebecca could not even celebrate a holiday with the entire family. Jacob and Esau remained separated for many years. I often think of the pain felt by their parents. It was many years later that we see the beautiful account of Jacob reaching out to Esau and making peace. Although the story ended in a beautiful way, there were many years in which the family missed out on unity—and who knows the pain of the parents?

Our response to these is not always healthy. We project the future without having enough information to give our projections accuracy—a host of "what if's." We consider the possibility of our own failure at parenting (when really, we were never the parents, nor could we provide guidance and influence equal to that of real parents).

Playing the Blame Game

Blaming others, would be doing Satan a favor. His job is to "steal, kill and destroy." (John 10:10) Then, we could blame God. Honestly, in desperation, we have considered this in times of extreme despair. That's the way it was in the time of Job. This same idea prevailed during the time of Christ. His disciples asked Him, "Rabbi, why was this man born blind? Was it because of his own sins or his parents?" John 9:3 is recorded in red letters because Jesus said it himself: "It was not because of his sins or his parent's sins. This happened, so the power of God could be seen in him."

Mother did a lot of good things, while raising her kids. One was to point us to good people to use as role models. That is the very message of Proverbs 2:20: "Walk in the steps of good men." Paul wrote, "You should imitate me as I imitate Christ." 1 Cor. 11:1. Let's be clear. Paul would not want us to imitate ALL that he did in life. He admitted in Romans 7 that he struggled with doing what he knew was right. However, in matters where he imitated Christ, he set a good example for us.

I never have wanted to be average. What is "not average?" I like the way T.D. Jakes put it: "Most people are manipulated by the approval of others, the paycheck that supports them and the lifestyle that has handcuffed them to the brass ring of perceived success."

Becoming a jock, cheerleader or honor student was out of the question.

(Whoever said these made a person above average?) It's interesting that when I get together at a high school reunion, we are not separated by what we were back then. It's what we've done with our lives since then that intrigues us, and the life experiences we endured to get us to where we are.

I find myself visiting with a classmate who now is showing clear evidence of Parkinson's Disease or physical signs of recent cancer treatment. I ask probing questions about these and the news I have heard about a child or other loved one being taken by death or experiencing great success. I'm not nosey. My values have changed since high school and we have more in common than ever before.

T.D. Jakes goes on to say "...at the end of the day, all that matters in this brief vacation we take on earth, is that we didn't shrink into a corner and waste the days we're given doing what we have to do rather than rising and taking on the challenge of becoming all we were created to be."

When we step up and seek to be above average, there are risks. A book I read over forty years ago left an image in my mind. Jess Lair wrote *I Ain't Much Baby, But I'm All I've Got*. He compared our desire for a good family, to how a fine-looking car might look in our driveway. It would be a collective pat on the back for us, if people could look at our children and be amazed at how well they have done in life. Perhaps we would impress those we know with our success as parents.

Collateral Damage

My mother shaped my thinking regarding my sister-in-law for many years of my life. Somehow, Mother had negative opinions of anyone who would marry one of her kids, (even my wife Brenda bore her judgment). She left this world at odds with my older sister's husband. I cannot think of anyone on the face of the earth who did as much for Mother as this man. But she just could not resolve her negative feelings toward him. Many of the issues were perceived rather than real.

Influenced by my mother, I grew up thinking that my brother's wife was some kind of witch. While stationed in Japan, I wrote her some pretty hurtful letters—even calling her names. However, it didn't stop her from showing kindness to me. She sent me books to read that I couldn't put down (reading was something I really struggled with in school). I read constantly now and have most of my adult life. I attribute this to Sandra.

After being discharged from the Navy, I traveled to Austin, Texas to see my brother and his family. I apologized to Sandra face to face, for all the hateful things I wrote to her. It was a big relief for me and a large burden off my heart.

I kept up with her through the years, making it a point to write, do and say things that communicated my appreciation for her. When she was placed in a nursing home, I visited her more than once. When she passed away, her daughters asked me to conduct her memorial service. The barriers had vanished, and I was honored to do so.

I never resented my mother for planting negative things in my mind. This woman endured a great deal in life. She provided guidance for my young sister and me.

That is the same with the "good men," to whom I was exposed. Mother demonstrated her wisdom, when she sent me to hang out with the son of our dentist. He was a man who practiced his faith. He provided for his family, treated his wife with respect and insisted on the best behavior from his sons. I didn't see that in my own home. I grew up wanting to be like this man in all his good ways. I spent a lot of time in the homes of other good families. I was there when the good dentist came home at the end of the day and watched how he greeted his wife and sons. I sat around the dinner table with the family and ate after he had given thanks.

The values I learned from these families provided a good deal of the subject matter for conversations Brenda and I had prior to marriage. I still am stunned at how similar her visions were to mine. They haven't changed in over fifty years.

Chapter 10

Random Kindness

"Is anyone alive to whom I can show God's kindness?" —2 Samuel 9:3

World War II brought changes that I can recall. In fact, it was not really a change for me. It was the world I came into. Experiencing a better world afterward was a change.

I knew rationing from the beginning. From 1942–1945, our country was focused on the war effort. Meat was rationed for families. Mother had metal tokens that were exchanged for a limited supply of meat at the grocery store. One butcher was very generous. He handed me a hot dog, every time I went with Mother to the store. I thought it was because I was such a cute little boy. Perhaps. His generosity and kindness made an impact on me.

Through junior high and high school, I worked at supermarkets. On the first day of my senior year, my employer called the school and left me a message. I was to report to the butcher shop, when I came to work that day. A promotion. No more sacking groceries and carrying them out in the hot/cold weather. I worked there my final year of school. What was lacking at home, was replaced in amazing ways. I now had more resources to participate in the financial needs at home.

Exposure to these extraordinary men continued into my adult life. There was the dairy farmer in Wisconsin. Brenda and I were stunned at the depth of his kindness.

We moved to Watertown, Wisconsin to build a church congregation from the ground up. This good man had inherited the farm from his dad. He was a young single man running this farm with the help of his mother. A young single lady moved there from another state to manage a retail chain store. She and the farmer proved a good match. After we had been there a while, our new friend gave his life completely to Christ. I had the privilege of baptizing him at a small nearby church. The baptistery was a steel cattle watering tank. How unique.

The couple bought their home as a kit, to be assembled on their property. Brenda and I spent many hours helping them build it, wearing out a few pairs of jeans in the process, especially on the roof.

We had no vacuum for our own home and finances were tight. A vacuum store in town allowed us to purchase a nice machine and pay over time. About halfway through the payment plan, I went to the store to make a payment. The person at the store informed me there was no balance—a kind dairy farmer had paid what was left.

There was a blinding snowstorm one winter. While the city was good about clearing the streets, all the snow was pushed in front of the driveways. We were snowed in. Early that morning, I heard a front loader (Bobcat) at work in our driveway. It was our friend. He just took it on himself to bring his farm machine to our house and clear a path for us to get our cars out.

A Heart for Kindness

It was this kind of kindness that changed Saul's heart toward David. In 1 Samuel 24, David crept into a cave where Saul was preoccupied. He certainly could have killed the king. Rather he "crept in unnoticed and cut off a corner of Saul's robe." (v.4) When Saul realized David could have killed him but didn't, he "wept aloud. You are more righteous than I...You have treated me well, but I have treated you badly." (v.17)

Two chapters later, we see the account of David taking Saul's spear and water jug from the ground next to his head as he slept. David's companions urged him to kill the King. They were convinced the Lord had delivered David's enemy into his hands. But David did not have the conscience for that.

When Saul realized that David had spared him a second time, he said "Come back home, my son, and I will no longer try to harm you, for you valued my life today. I have been a fool and very, very wrong." (vs. 21)

It Does Matter

Our public school distributed signs for citizens to display in their yards, in an effort to address the problem of bullying. The signs simply say, KINDNESS MATTERS. Having been on the receiving end of this issue, I can testify to the truth of that declaration.

I love the account of David and Mephibosheth. I encouraged my children to name one of their boys Mephibosheth. No takers on that one.

Mephibosheth was the son of David's friend Jonathan, son of King Saul. He was five, when his nurse fell while running with the boy in her arms and Mephibosheth became disabled. (2 Samuel 4) When David became king, he asked if his deceased friend Jonathan had anyone still alive from the family "to whom I can show God's kindness?" (2 Samuel 9:3) When he was told about Mephibosheth (lame in both feet) David vowed to him "Don't be afraid, for I will surely show you kindness for the sake of your father Jonathan. I will restore to you all the land that belonged to your grandfather Saul, and you will always eat at my table." (2 Samuel 9:7)

David certainly did a lot wrong, but this account moves my heart. David is my example, when I am moved to reach out to a veteran who is alone in life, except for the people in the senior living facility where he lives. All day he repeats the words "thank you," even for the smallest kindness shown him. I have twice taken him somewhere, so we both can eat at one of his favorite restaurants in town. It's quite a chore. His walker is so big, it barely fits in my trunk. He moves slowly. Getting in and out of the car, is a big deal. I am lifted by our time together. It is worth every minute. There are many lonely people out there. I'm not King David, but I can identify with his heart of kindness. Thank God I married a woman who has the same heart. Brenda and I have been known to tip the waiter/waitress a little more than we should.

We learned how to receive and be grateful. If it is more blessed to give than to receive (Acts 20:35), we can get a clear picture of that principle by being a receiver every once in a while. We also learned that kindness does not need permission. If there is a need and I have the means to provide a solution, then that is what I need to do. (1 John 3:17, James 2:15. Proverbs 19:17, Matthew 25:35–40)

Isn't it uplifting, when kindness is shown? It helps to offset the evil that is around us.

Chapter 11

How Pain Comes

*"We are not necessarily doubting that God will do the best for us;
we are wondering how painful the best will turn out to be."* —C.S. Lewis

Every day the media publishes accounts of a person who has ruined his life and that of his victim(s). Their photo or mugshot is splashed across newspapers and TV screens. I am filled with grief over the hurt that story represents. I also think of the parents of that individual, who are looking at the same photo. It is impossible to put myself in their place and feel what they are feeling. My heart cannot muster that much empathy.

We are aware of those who make bad, impulsive and selfish choices that bring harm to others. The victims commonly are those whose lives were snuffed out or endured permanent damage. I am often brought face to face with these offenders, as they are being detained by police officers, handcuffed or on the way to jail, as they ride in the back seat of the police car.

Seeing someone bring pain to another person, can generate emotions of judgment and despair. I experienced neglect and abandonment in my own family. I lost count of the number of times I visited Dad in jail. He left an abundance of tools, when he passed. I know that many of them were stolen from hardware stores. Once, as he was being escorted into jail (before metal detectors) he pulled his pistol out and fired it in the elevator, leaving a significant dent in the side of the elevator (it may still be there, but I choose not to look).

I loved him and repeatedly told him so, yet his agenda often was more important than those around him (even those who loved him).

The direction I took boils down to this:

1. I didn't choose him as my father. God did that and there is something in scripture about honoring father and mother.

2. I don't have to pattern my life after ANYONE'S negative example.

I am a bit distraught that the dreams Brenda and I share haven't completely come true, as we envisioned. We are facing the rest of our lives differently than that for which we worked and prayed. It is what it is—at least that's what I'm told. I cannot change it. I am confident I will be made better, by living through the disappointment. As I listen to others, I learn that we are not alone. Frequent funeral services have been added to my preaching opportunities. Each time, I am reminded how much life changes, when death separates us from someone who has been a part of our life. It even goes deeper, because the entire world changes as each person leaves. The dynamic changes and we are in a constant state of adjustment, as people we know leave the world and others enter it.

Biblical Fathers and Sons

We find an emotional scene in 2 Samuel 18. David has escaped harm from the rebellion of his own son. He now receives what most people would consider "good news." Absalom is no longer a threat—he is dead. Yet David was "overcome with emotion. He went to the room over the gateway and burst into tears. As he went, he cried, "O my son Absalom! My son, my son Absalom! If only I had died instead of you! O Absalom, my son, my son."

David envisioned his son growing up and legitimately assuming a leadership position of the nation. Assembling a following of rebels and seeking to overthrow his father, could not have been a part of David's dreams for his son.

Eli's sons served as priests of God. 1 Samuel 3:13 declares that "his sons are blaspheming God and he hasn't disciplined them." Hophni and Phinehas, the two sons of Eli, were killed in a battle with the Philistines. (1 Samuel 4:11) At the news that the Ark of God had been captured and his sons were dead, Eli "fell backward from his seat, broke his neck and died." (Verse 18) The passage goes on to mention the wife of Phinehas going into labor and dying during childbirth. It is stunning to witness such a reaction to bad news regarding a loved one. It happens somewhere every day.

Loving Others like Family

Two longtime friends called in the past few days. Both have had a reoccurrence of cancer. They have both been told it likely would be terminal. They also both told me they wanted me to conduct their memorial service, when the time came.

That was a first for me. I am usually contacted by the family, after the person passes. In over forty years of ministry, this is the first time I have been asked directly by the person himself. It was difficult and an honor at the same time. Our final visits and the memorial still carry painful memories. There is an empty spot in my heart with them gone, yet I look forward to seeing them again.

Jake was the first one to pass. He reminded me of the time that his brother was randomly murdered in an apartment parking lot. I lived through that experience, simply by listening. He followed the investigation and the trial and admitted that he didn't do well during that time. I can vouch for that from the many visits we had during the experience. He either would call me to diffuse or I would call him for a progress report on his emotions. It was the same Jake I had known, only with a very heavy heart. He knew the scriptures, as well as anyone. Why can't we just assure ourselves of God's promises and brush off the effects of such events? Is it a lack of faith on our part?

On the same day I spoke with Jake, I heard from a third friend. He is 50 and I have known him since he was eighteen. His son and one of my grandsons are less than a week apart in age and have the same first name. When we spoke, I knew he was being treated for throat cancer, although he never smoked or used anything that would normally cause that condition.

Another friend went with me to visit the 50-year-old in the hospital.

Afterward, he invited me to his house for a family dinner. I was far from home and shaken by our hospital visit. We were discussing the occurrence of these "off the charts" challenges in life. He mentioned a gentleman at church who had moved to a nursing home, long before he should have. Cancer had taken the lives of his two daughters. This was followed by the same experience with his wife. He was not prepared to be alone.

My dinner host told me long ago that his brother was randomly shot and killed. It is difficult for me to fathom this same experience with two of my favorite people.

Listening to them, is all I can offer. It's not a grand gesture, but often it's all I have. It must have been meaningful to them. They continued to tell me the story over and over. It has been stunning to watch them (and others) feel safe enough to also share with me other struggles. I need that kind of safe place as well. I want to be a safe place for others.

Chapter 12

Amazing Pain

"For I am convinced that neither death nor life, neither angels nor demons, neither the present nor the future, nor any powers, neither height nor depth, nor anything else in all creation, will be able to separate us from the love of God that is in Christ Jesus our Lord." —Romans 8:38–39

The police call it a "disturbance" and sometimes a "domestic." If it involves family, it is termed "domestic disturbance." An elderly gentleman called 911. He had been robbed and roughed up—by his grandson. I was on scene with officers who were talking with the family and gathering information. The sergeant radioed that he had detained the suspect one street away and the rest of us hurried there. The young man was handcuffed, placed in a police car and transported to jail.

While we were at the residence, the grandfather was receiving attention from ambulance attendants. My heart led me to this elderly gentleman. However, he was surrounded by those caring for him. I spoke with one of his daughters and assured her of prayer on behalf of the family. This is not the behavior that a grandfather anticipates from a grandchild. We don't need to search far for evidence, that the world we live in is broken.

One evening, a man approached an officer and me and requested that we take him. His record revealed ample evidence that an arrest was appropriate. He was handcuffed and placed in the back seat of the police car for the ride downtown. The officer slid the window open and we talked the entire twenty minutes. He admitted a serious drug addiction and wanted help. He had an altercation with a friend over something foolish. When someone is in a position of submission, it is often a great time to have a serious discussion. At least, I give it a shot. I discuss with them the opportunity this experience can offer. It can be an opportunity to change their actions and their direction. Loving themselves as much as others love them, often gives them the motivation that they need to rewrite the script of their lives. Consideration must be given to the loved ones of the person who caused the damage. Someone loves that person, even though he/she makes choices that hurt those who love them.

What's Behind the Badge?

I have not found bigger hearts anywhere, than those of police officers.

We were transporting a young mother from a retail store for shoplifting. She was caught by store security (after putting up a fight) and detained. We talked about her children who were staying with an older couple. As we pulled up to the jail, the officer called the couple and explained the situation. He asked to put the children on the phone. First, he spoke with them and gently explained that their mom had made some mistakes. He told them that she would be dealing with the results of her mistakes for a time. He put the mother on speaker phone, so she could talk to her children. After she was booked, we drove to where the children were and sat down with them to talk. The officer never spoke despairingly of their mother. He assured them that she loved them and wanted to protect and provide for them. We encouraged them to be patient with their mother and love her in return. It is one of many experiences that I will remember for years to come.

I have read interviews with the parents of some of the worst offenders. No one discounted their love for the individual. It is in that context that we begin to understand the love God has for us. We cannot misbehave enough to turn God against us. That is Paul's message in Romans 8:37–39. It is a recurring theme in exploring changes in the life of a person who thinks "I've been so bad God couldn't possibly forgive me." It is comforting to know that God's thoughts are not our thoughts. (Isaiah 55:8)

It is stunning to read a victim's impact statement, after a court conviction. What is anticipated most is a statement of extreme pain at the hurt or loss of a loved one at the hands of the one convicted. It is not uncommon to hear these individuals express bitterness toward the offender—wishing him a miserable future. That is difficult enough to take in. We cannot even begin to feel the hurt that person is feeling. However, there is another victim that deserves consideration. It is the loved ones of the one convicted; the parents, grandparents and siblings. These people invested significant effort into the lives of this individual, envisioning a better outcome. They are now feeling that their efforts have been rejected. This person chose a totally different path for themselves. At this point, it is irreversible.

Recently, I read of a man in his early twenties. If his life is not ruined, it will be significantly hindered for many years. His parents are in a position of leadership. The comments on social media suggested that the parents should leave their positions. My question is why? What is it about his failures that can be blamed on the parents? I can say from experience that the temptation to take responsibility is there. What do we do with that? It makes no sense to impose additional loss. That is exactly what Satan wants. (John 10:10) Let's put things in perspective this way: "God is the father of all mankind. Do bad choices by God's children make Him a failure?"

There is an account of another young man in a responsible and honored profession, who did some horrible things. For his crimes, he received a prison sentence in excess of 200 years. The article showed his father in the courtroom, waiting for the judge to pronounce sentence. I feel like I am looking at a bottomless well. Who can fathom the pain that this father will live with each day, until he takes his final breath?

We are shocked when someone well-known and loved surfaces with a different picture. Consider the accounts of famous politicians, ministers, business leaders, sports figures, educators or celebrities who have chosen an adverse path. Do we need to recall the news coverage? We hear comments from the public that this individual has violated the admiration we had for who we thought that person was. Part of our own life is wiped out. What about those closest to them?

The news released a video of several teenage boys doing some very terrible things—destroying property and hurting people. Their parents reported them to the authorities. That took courage.

Another twist to this, are the mental and emotional challenges to children of the offenders. I spoke with a young mother, who reaches out to females caught up in sexual abuse. She explained that her own father is spending the rest of his life in prison for abusing children in horrible ways.

In a recent article regarding the suicide of a sixteen-year-old girl, the father made some suggestions about being observant of the child's changes of behavior and urged parents not to pressure the child into superior performance. In the article, Dr. Michael Rosen stated, "The most difficult thing I have to treat are the parents of children who have committed suicide." Again, I am baffled at the life-changing choices made by a person. It overwhelms my emotions to think of the pain endured by those who loved that person.

Holding on to Hope

The apostle Paul spoke with hope in the verse mentioned in the beginning of this chapter. Fifty plus years of marriage have helped to keep Brenda and me on the same page. We both have experienced the death of parents, a sibling and a grandchild. We have experienced job loss, undesirable choices by children and grandchildren we share and the consequences of our own mistakes. Our faith has been shaken—but not lost. Together and separately, we seek to impart the message of Paul to those we touch: "nothing can separate us from the love of God which is in Christ Jesus."

Chapter 13

Less Than Desired

"The son shall not bear the iniquities of the father; neither shall the father bear the iniquities of the son." —Ezekiel 18:20

"and he (Jacob) was limping because of the injury to his hip" —Genesis 32:30

It is not my thinking that is flawed. It is the response of my heart and Satan knows that. I read a statement a few years ago that rocked my world. John Eldridge wrote "Did it ever cross your mind that every thought that crosses your mind is not your own?" By nature, I am a worrier. It came from my mother. It remains one negative childhood trait, that I haven't been able to dispel completely. My mother is not to blame. I claim full responsibility. I know that worry is not right.

Job must have been a bit of a worrier. In the midst of his suffering, he declared, "What I feared has come upon me." (Job 3:25,26) Although Mother has been gone a long time, those of us who knew her best, know that she dealt with a great deal of pain in her life. I learned some survival skills from her regarding dealing with hardship. However, she could "what if" better than anyone I know. By the time she projected the outcome of a scenario, I had heard all the possibilities—and none of them were good. Some of the pain I have endured was caused by my failures—but not all of it. We are not perfect, and I never would insist I did everything right.

Like most parents, we poured our hearts out on all our children and grandchildren. It was the subject of endless conversations between Brenda and me, when we spent time on dates. This even occurred when we were parked in the car in a secluded place. We just committed that if we married, we would not repeat the distance we both experienced from our parents and grandparents. A lot went missing and we were determined not to repeat the cycle.

I must pause here and make allowances for parents and perhaps even grandparents. A person cannot give what he/she does not have. Ultimately, we are responsible for our own success or failure.

Ezekiel 18:20 captured my attention long ago, "The son shall not bear the iniquities of the father; neither shall the father bear the iniquities of the son. The soul that sins, it shall die." We have a choice and can decide to live a different way. Even if we do, we might walk with a limp.

I always have loved the account of Jacob wrestling with an angel—overcoming him. (Genesis 32:22-32, Hosea 12:4) Three things result from this contest: 1. Jacob's name was changed to "Israel," while his contender refused to reveal his name; 2. Israel receives a blessing from this experience and 3. Israel is left with a hip out of joint, which caused him to limp throughout the rest of his life. We can reject a repeat of the environment in which we were raised. That is exactly the commitment Brenda and I made, even before we married.

The idea of walking with a limp is intriguing. Paul endured a physical issue that God refused to remove. God said, "My power is made perfect in weakness." I've attended AA meetings with friends. When a person introduces himself, he says "Hi, my name is Bill and I am an alcoholic." I've never heard an alcoholic claim complete deliverance. There is a clear admission that they are only one drink away from falling off the wagon. Strength and support get them through, but the propensity still is there. They walk with a limp. Translate that into issues with just about any addiction (drugs, pornography, tobacco, prescription medication). Taking up our cross is a daily effort, (Luke 9:23) He never leaves us to walk alone but clearly demonstrates His power in weakness. (2 Corinthians 12:9)

My Metaphorical Limp

I carried resentment for years. I found it very difficult to speak favorably of my father. He made life difficult for us, by drinking and being unfaithful to our mother. I forgave him for those things long ago. It was not for his benefit, but for mine. He did pass on to me some good qualities. I have developed them and made them a part of my character.

I was convinced that I was a disappointment to my father. My brother entered the Marines and went to Korea during the war. He came back and became a veterinarian. Dad had a right to be proud of his oldest son. I was proud too. My brother knew how much leadership I missed at home and gave me a great deal of encouragement. It took a while to find my way, but I eventually became a minister. For a father who resented religion, the church and equated the Bible with Aesop's Fables, I fell out of his favor with my career choice.

My father had a strong dislike for church. As a young boy in parochial school, a teacher took a toy away from him. Furious, he stormed out of class, grabbed his young sister by the arm and led her out. He never returned.

Dad was involved in a wreck on his motor scooter. He fell and was severely scratched by the pavement and gravel. I was young but horrified by his injuries. When he learned he was in a hospital supported by a church, he insisted on going home—immediately.

When my brother graduated from veterinary college, the entire family packed up and drove to attend his graduation. There were many graduates from Texas A & M. It was a very long wait, just to watch one person walk across the stage and receive his diploma.

I finished college with a degree in biblical studies. My mother came to Oklahoma to my graduation and attended along with my wife and our oldest daughter Holly. Two and a half years later, I completed a master's degree at a graduate school of Theology in Memphis, Tennessee. My mother took the bus from Texas to attend, along with a sweet lady from the church which Brenda and I served in Mississippi. My wife was there, along with our daughter (and now a son). My college graduation did not receive the same attention from the family, as that of my brother. That pulled at my heart for years, but I got over it —kind of. I suppose that is one of the ways I walk with a limp. My head knows that God ultimately is the scorekeeper. His validation is what counts. My heart is pulled along to adopt that same truth. Brenda has been there all along and validated my every effort. When I received my master's degree, the school presented her with a PHT diploma that stood for "Putting Hubby Through." How appropriate is that?

Sweet Memories

Our granddaughter reminds us of the approaching birthdays of her three boys, by saying, "I'm not ready for him to turn three" (or whatever age they will be). Brenda and I built the early years of our marriage around three young children. As with most parents, memories of them developing are precious. Reflecting on those days, I once penned a poem entitled "Memories in the Walls."

When this house shall become silent
And independence calls.
Precious treasures will sustain us
With memories in the walls.

When we search the place for loved ones
And encounter silent halls.
We'll hear all the sounds of growing
From the memories in the walls.

Though the echoes will sound lonely
When the dusk of our life calls.
We'll find strength to journey forward
From the memories in the walls.

We've toiled to urge them onward
Picked them up from all their falls.

Kissed their hurts and made them better
  Now it's memories in the walls.

When thoughts are brought to visit
  By the tractors and the dolls.
We spend a few quiet moments
  With the memories in the walls.

When it's time to sing our anthem
  And our greatness none recalls.
We'll know our greatest purpose
  From the memories in the walls.

This mother was only four, when her brother was found unresponsive in his crib. She was joined in counseling for a time by others with similar experiences. Being a wife and mother is now ingrained in her soul. Her boys join with their dad and bless her. (Proverbs 31:28) From the vantage point of grandparents, we know we have not LOST a grandson. We know where he is.

She is married to a dedicated husband and father. The three boys have been encouraged to love their great-grandparents—showering us with affection. We witness the development of good and sustaining values. That is certainly on the list of benefits from the event that traumatized our family many years ago. We did not see any benefits at the time. A heart overwhelmed by pain rarely does.

Chapter 14

The Tie That Binds

"I have learned how to be content with whatever I have. I know how to live on almost nothing or with everything. I have learned the secret of living in every situation, whether it is with a full stomach or empty, with plenty or little. For I can do everything through Christ, who gives me strength."
—Philippians 4:13

Do we set ourselves up for disappointment, by creating expectations that we have no right to create? For most of my adult years, I have studied and learned that "unmet expectations" is a significant cause for failure in relationships. My major professor in graduate school was not even a professor of marriage and family counseling, but I learned a significant principle from him. This good teacher contended that "marriages don't fail—people fail." I have found that truth to hold in just about every kind of relationship involving two or more human beings.

My favorite pre-marital counseling question to a couple is, "Why do you want to get married?" Almost every time it is "Because we love one another." Or "We have so much in common." I gently and kindly ask them to recall their answers to my question a few years down the road. Will that love hold firm, after the first child is born, hormonal changes occur, a child makes bad choices or attention is focused on an ill and dying parent, grandparent or sibling? These are situations that have the potential to upstage commitment. It can be a time of testing for a relationship.

Real Life Testing

As I write this, Brenda, our daughter Amber, and I are at the cancer center. We come at least once a week—sometimes more. Every third visit consists of Brenda receiving chemotherapy. The room contains over 20 lounge chairs usually filled with cancer patients sharing the same experience. We spend a large amount of time talking with other patients and their families, who have been doing this much longer. So far, we have not met a single person who has chosen to give up.

Fifty plus years of marriage has yielded Brenda and me some good years. Of course, it has not been without challenges.

Following surgery on her eyes in January, Brenda noticed other symptoms. With the thought that it might be a reaction to the recent surgery, we made a late-night visit to the emergency room. The doctor did x-rays and found nothing. A sonogram revealed large stones in her gallbladder. The ER doctor stressed the importance of getting this taken care of—soon.

I had seen a surgeon regarding a hernia and planned a repair. The next morning after Brenda's ER visit, I called the office of my surgeon to ask if he did surgery on gallbladders. They saw her within two days. Convinced that more was going on, we were sent for a CT scan, which revealed enlarged lymph nodes in the abdomen.

Brenda was very ill and admitted into the hospital through the ER. A needle biopsy was done. She had lymphoma. While she was having her gallbladder removed, surgeons also did a bone marrow biopsy and installed a port through her chest wall.

She was given her first round of chemotherapy, while in the hospital. We took her home. The next day we made a follow-up visit to the office of the oncologist. The chemotherapy had totally depleted her white blood cells. That evening, her temperature rose considerably. I called the oncologist that night. He instructed us to take her to the ER and that she likely would be admitted.

Brenda claims Philippians 4:13 as her favorite scripture. I have heard it used a lot in times of distress. That's exactly how Paul used it, as he wrote his letter. He pointed out how his life had been affected by his ministry. "I have learned how to be content with whatever I have. I know how to live on almost nothing or with everything. I have learned the secret of living in every situation, whether it is with a full stomach or empty, with plenty or little. For I can do everything through Christ, who gives me strength." The strength of Christ is not what empowers one to climb Mount Everest or win a NASCAR championship or PGA tournament. The context here is living with what life deals us.

It gets my attention when I am talking with a person who is receiving chemo and says, "I'm terminal." This person knows the outcome of the disease. However, they are doing what they can to get the most out of what life has left for them.

It Never Quits

Recently I was speaking with a man (probably in his fifties) who is a joy to be around. He was sitting in a recliner just across from Brenda. He explained that his illness is terminal. His attitude was not. He was talking, laughing and looking things up on his iPad. He explained that he had been talking with others, before I walked up. He had been asking this question: "If you could write a book about your life, what would the title be?" Although this was a while back, I still think about it. He explained that he listens constantly for what it is God wants him to learn from his experience. I told him that (as a caregiver) I am doing the same thing. I know that more than one voice speaks to me. I spend a lot of time trying to discern which voice to tune in and which to reject. He heartily agreed with me on that point.

These patients are often very young. Their stories are intriguing. No one has given up. Everyone expresses hope. Most are surrounded by family, either by their chair or in the waiting area nearby. They have learned to deal with the situation they face and not be jerked around by an unwelcomed experience.

We are learning a new meaning to the above passage. We have held the hand of family members and close friends, as they endured the same thing. Whatever we may face, someone nearby has faced the same experience and have the power to comfort.

In Philippians 4:13, Paul is not relating times of superhuman strength. He explains that he has lived with much and he has lived with little. Romans 8 (also written by Paul) speaks of our groaning. Certain experiences make us groan. David had every reason to groan. He was confronted by Nathan the prophet and heard the ugly truth. (2 Samuel 12) He had committed adultery, Bathsheba was pregnant. David arranged for the death of her husband. Uriah was a loyal soldier in David's army—how did he deserve that? The baby born to Bathsheba died. David was the one who deserved to die. However, he played a crucial role in maintaining the throne that Christ would eventually occupy.

Where was the fairness? There is a married woman who was misused by a lustful king who had the power to do so. Her husband was killed, and her baby died. There were plenty of reasons to groan. It was strength from Christ that provided Paul with the ability to be encouraged, whether things were going well or not. That is the context of this passage.

In 2 Corinthians 6, he describes some of these experiences. "We patiently endure troubles, hardships, and calamities of every kind. We have been beaten, put in prison, faced angry mobs, worked to exhaustion, endured sleepless nights and gone without food." How did he stay positive through this? (Philippians 4:13)

In 1 Corinthians 16:9, this same Paul describes his work in Ephesus: "Here is a wide-open door for a great work here, although many oppose me." Opposition is something Paul expected. He considered it an opportunity to accomplish more. Smooth sailing likely would not. Where did he get his courage to continue even in the middle of opposition? (Philippians 4:13)

Chapter 15

How Are You?

"Don't tell your friends about your indigestion. How are you is a greeting, not a question." —Arthur Guiterman

"How are you?" That is the southern way to greet someone. Most of the time, the response is "Fine," even if things are not fine. Who wants to be less than fine? Someone in AA might answer "It's a good day to be sober." There is more to that question than most people realize. The person who asks, is not really fishing for me to list everything that is troubling me. Most of the time they turn and give their attention to something (or someone) else and don't even listen long enough to hear my reply.

I have some interesting ways to respond to that question.

1. Often, I just don't respond at all and watch how quickly they become occupied with something else.

2. I will say "I don't know yet."

3. "Compared to what."

4. "I woke up thing morning."

5. "I'm getting better."

The officer and I enter the home of a family, who had been caring for the man of the house. He had liver failure and had quit breathing. All efforts of the first responders failed. He was in his mid-forties. It added to my evaluation of the time I am given. The officer and I walked away, listening to the wife crying very loudly. His daughters also were in tears. The remains of the husband, father and grandfather were on the floor next to his bed. He was too young, but (according to his family) his choices had contributed to the illness that took his life. The choices he made for himself had been sealed and affected people who loved him. The family would go forward with the memories they had—whatever they were.

One friend shared his story. He had been married for twenty years, when his wife was diagnosed with cancer. In the midst of that illness, she informed him that their marriage had reached the end. He told me he had learned that, in such cases, the divorce rate skyrockets. Those who have longevity are at far less risk. My friend could not point to a cause of the breakdown, yet he cared for his wife in her illness. Years later, he still is at a loss to understand or explain it.

Brenda and I recall more than one suicide attempt by our son. On one of them, she placed him in the car, drove at high speed with flashers on and was stopped by a police officer. She explained the situation and the officer gave her an escort to the hospital. He has reached the point, where another such attempt would be highly unlikely. We are grateful that he is better mentally and emotionally. Yet, we still recall the pain.

I cannot think through this, without recalling the experience of a couple who became dear friends years ago. This loving couple had two children. They were awakened by a fire in their house. They escaped. Watching their burning house with their two children still inside, instinct led the father in that direction. That area was totally engulfed in flames and those standing by restrained him. The children did not survive.

The father was a bitter man for a while and wanted no more children. His wife felt differently. She intentionally allowed herself the opportunity to conceive and a child was born. He learned to love that new child with a special love. To see him love his new child, was a stretch from the life of pain and bitterness he felt from his previous experience. The couple entered the ministry and accomplished some great things.

I recall a good man from my first full-time preaching job. He was a faithful and active member of the congregation and influenced his family in good ways. He was one of the "good men" that we read about in Proverbs 2:20. An employee of the county maintaining roads, he drove one of the large road graders that kept the gravel roads smooth. He did it for years without incident. Once, when he was backing his large tractor, a child on a bicycle ventured behind the machine and this good man failed to see him. The child lost his life and my friend would be haunted for life. He was skilled at running this machine and no negligence was involved. His gentle spirit was unmistakable. He spent his days looking for something he could do for others, rather than waiting to be asked.

Driving Cattle

Our family moved to northern Mississippi in 1972 to work with a small church. It was in a community of dairy farms. It was not uncommon to come home and find a sack of fresh corn, a watermelon, cantaloupe, tomatoes, onions, carrots or radishes by the door. It was a treat to receive these things, without having to do the gardening that went along with it.

One member invited me to his large cattle ranch. He put me on a horse (not a big deal since I had been around horses all my life). He asked me to help drive cattle from one pasture to another. That was a first. The interesting thing was that this gentleman walked the whole time, while I rode. It seemed awesome that he was willing to do that.

This was a real mentor. Another member had hunting dogs and invited me to hunt birds with him. It became addictive and I still love to do that today. A man (or woman) can never know the lasting effect of his/her influence. Influence is a certainty. It either will be positive or negative. It never will be zero. It is a reflection of how God brought His son to earth, emptied Him of His divinity (Philippians 2:7) and made him an example to us. (John 13:15)

Real Life Application Is Not Without Challenge

I was reading the parable of the Pharisee and Publican. I confess that I have looked at the church bulletin with a similar attitude, as the Pharisee saw the Publican. I have checked to see who is in the hospital or who is facing a new illness. I then express gratitude that I am not on that list. Our family is healthy and well.

Brenda and I spent several days in the hospital with our infant daughter following surgery for a Craniosynostosis. Amber's roommate was a young girl who was there when we came and remained when we left. She was being tested for Lyme disease. Brenda and the girl's mother talked endlessly. Later we corresponded by mail with the mom of that little girl and were assured she recovered. The effort to keep in touch was worth it.

I met a lady who told me she was a book editor. I mentioned to her that I was writing a book. She asked me what it was about, and I explained, "Off the charts pain and suffering and how we may or may not deal with it." She asked for a summary. I stated that we cannot be pharisaic about the suffering of others who have it worse than us. She replied, "Let me tell you our story." I braced for this one.

She and her husband have a daughter who became sick with a very large tumor barely into her teens. Because hospitals were crowded, they were sent to a children's hospital miles away. There they encountered other children being treated for cancer. When they were informed that their daughter had a benign and removable tumor, she was grateful, knowing full well that other parents were not receiving the same good news. She had formed a relationship with the mother of her daughter's roommate. They were dismissed and went home while the other mother waited for the diagnoses of her child. Not following up with that mother has given her something to think about for years.

Back in 1992, I was going through a reflective point in my life. This motivated me to write down many of my thoughts. I had been mentored in life and business by a person who I consider a great man. No, he didn't do everything right. Who does? The perfection of Jesus earned Him the right to be the savior of mankind.

My mentor had an amazing biography. He grew up on a farm, served in the navy and earned an undergraduate and graduate degree with income from being a barber. He taught school, coached students in poetry competitions and had a poem of his own placed in the Kennedy Library. This good man entered the insurance business late in his life and preached until his death. I was not initially assigned to him. However, someone above us both concluded that I was a certain failure and placed me under a new man's leadership. I was inspired to write down what was in my heart. He made some favorable comments on this piece, when he read it. That made me proud.

The Reaper Speaks

The reaper makes his daily rounds
　　to this good earth below.
And frequently with those he's found
　　I see someone I know.

He speaks to me when he comes near
　　I often hear him say
"I'm not the one whom you should fear
　　It's not your turn today."

"Treasure life" his voice is felt,
　　"and let this be a clue.
Today I'm here for someone else,
　　Someday I'll come for you."

The reaper makes his daily rounds
　　And makes sure that I know
That where he leads me time abounds
　　But now's the time to grow.

I know a couple who has faced illness with their oldest son. He was diagnosed with cancer as an infant. How do we wrap our hearts around such a situation? Is it possible that we become pharisaical and say, "I thank God my family is not facing that?"

Where Is God in All This?

Although God has the power to bring an end to pain and emotional trauma, he allowed His son to suffer at the hands of cruel people and give His life unjustly as He, as a loving father, watched. When He speaks, we can be assured that He speaks from experience. We are not feeling anything He has not felt.

It is a real turn-off to use my experience as an open door to elaborate on another person. I often feel like chopped liver. I can't even count the times I have had someone ask how things are going with the illness we face and take very little time to listen to my response. When I pause at the end of my comments, there is an immediate response of a personal experience or that of someone they know. Often the situation they describe is far worse than ours. It is refreshing and comforting, when someone focuses on me, listens intently to what I say, then asks questions for clarity. At that moment, I feel like the most important person in the world—at least to that person. He is totally focused on my response.

It is often unclear what a person means when they say, "I'll be praying for you." It would be much more meaningful to hear them say something like "My wife and I were praying this morning and specifically asked God to ban the bad cells that have entered your wife's body. We also asked God to give you hope, comfort, and strength, because we know He loves you." I don't want to judge anyone who says, "I'll be praying for you," I've said it too. Then I got busy with my own affairs and didn't remember to mention the person to whom I committed.

It is a puzzle to explain different outcomes to our requests. Even Jesus said to the Father "If it be possible, let this cup pass from me." However, it was not possible. Jesus knew how history had pointed to the event He was about to face. His request for another way demonstrated His humanity.

In graduate school, I studied apologetics. A large part of this subject is to produce evidence for the existence of God and inspiration of scripture. I learned that the hardest argument to deal with from atheists, is the existence of evil, especially the presence of pain and suffering. The argument of an atheist is "You are saying God is all good and all powerful, yet evil continues to exist in this world and your God does nothing to do away with it. Human suffering continues to exist in this world and your God (whom you say is all powerful) does nothing to eliminate it.

Mother's Relief

The plane landed at Edwards Air Force Base in California. It was a 36-hour trip from Tachikawa Japan. The length of the trip was partially due to the engine trouble between Honolulu and the mainland. We returned to Honolulu, changed planes and left again.

It was cold in Northern California, even in August, but no one cared. We were on U.S. soil. After two years in Japan, home dominated our thoughts. One fellow passenger dropped to his knees and kissed the ground. I was more interested in getting to a telephone. I made the collect call to Mother. When she heard my voice, she began to sob very loudly. I braced myself for bad news. When I asked what was wrong, she said, "I've had two sons go overseas and both of them came home safely." That gave me some insight into what my mother had prayed for, while I was gone. I know there were other parents, who prayed for the safe return of their sons, but to no avail. I cannot explain it.

At the end of our first year in a two-year intense ministerial training program, the teacher who was going to walk us through Job next year came into our classroom for an introduction. He told us his plans for that class after the summer break. Then he gave us the assignment to read Job ten times during the summer, in preparation for that class. By the end of the summer, I felt like part of Job's family.

Brenda and I have refocused on how to respond to someone who is going through a hard time. I have one friend who asks specific questions and when I am through talking, he grabs my hand and prays aloud right where we stand. Brenda tells me that when she hears of someone facing any kind of trial, she immediately lifts them up in prayer. From now on, I will have no problem asking a person questions like "How did you feel when you first learned of this?" Then I will make eye contact with that person and listen until he/she finishes talking. I thank God for that lesson.

If we didn't love the people around us, we would not hurt when they hurt. Brenda and I have hurt deeply, as we watched one or more of our children or grandchildren make life choices that will leave them facing dire consequences. We have prayed separately and together, until it seemed we had run out of words to take our requests to God. I recall studying Romans 8 in a college class. The verse was 26 "The Holy Spirit prays for us with groaning that cannot be expressed in words." By studying that passage in the original language, we learned that when we lift our hearts to God in sincere prayer, we are not alone. We have the Holy Spirit interceding alongside us.

The vision we left class with that day was that we grab one end of the table, the Holy Spirit grabs the other end and we lift together. In bringing our sincere requests before God on behalf of someone we love, we are comforted knowing we had help, even though we often feel that our own words are inadequate. In fact, when we can't come up with words that are appropriate, it is okay. God can hear our hearts, even without words. He is amazing.

I am okay if you don't ask me "how are you?" Just say "nice to see you, Tom."

Chapter 16

Motivation to Continue

"Direct your children onto the right path, and when they are older,
they will not leave it." —Proverbs 22:6

Expectations test a relationship, when it comes to raising children. I met a school resource officer who told me about the kinds of illegal drugs confiscated from the middle school students, with whom he spends his days. I was stunned. He said it also goes on among second graders as well. He went on to explain that he had confiscated a serious illegal drug from a student, who was given the drug by his father.

Early in my ministry, I led a discussion at church regarding what I had learned about rearing children. Only two of our three children had been born at the time. They were very young, and we still were learning. The discussion centered on Proverbs 22:6: "Direct your children onto the right path, and when they are older, they will not leave it." Sounds like some kind of guarantee, doesn't it? How do we explain Ezekiel 18:20: "The child will not be punished for the parent's sins, and the parent will not be punished for the child's sins?"

During our discussion, a well-meaning church lady spoke up and declared that "Raising children is like buttoning a shirt. If you start out with the right button, the task will conclude the way it should." In the beginning of my ministry, I envisioned myself somewhat of an authority on child-rearing. I was convinced that the right efforts would end in the right results. If this were true, then God's own effort at being a father to mankind would be questionable. Look at the bad choices made by humans, when we had the ultimate parent from the beginning.

Where's the Child-Rearing Manual?

Jess Lair pointed out that "we cannot raise a child. We only can sponsor them." I have heard Proverbs 22:6 explained in this way: "…train up a child according to his natural bent." One of my fellow students in preaching school has a daughter the same age as our oldest daughter. His daughter was born deaf. She and our daughter were friends and played together. Holly picked up on sign language and wanted to learn more. When she was twelve, I drove Holly into Minneapolis from our home just inside Wisconsin (about 60 miles) and we both attended a class on sign language. When that class was over, there were no other classes. However, the interest never left her. Many years later, one of her daughters is focused on learning sign language, as her other language at school. It takes some careful observation to determine the "natural bent" of our children. Let's be honest. This is not a passage guaranteeing a child's proper spiritual choices in life. It would be nice, but it just is not the case.

Who is accountable? By inspiration, the Apostle Paul firmly puts the blame where it belongs. "All have sinned and fall short of the glory of God." (Romans 3:23) God can't be blamed for that. Neither can good, godly parents always be blamed for the adverse life choices of their children. I made a few unfortunate choices in my life that I regret. These were contrary to what my mother had taught me. I cannot blame her for my negative choices or the consequences. I made certain she never learned about some of them. I am thankful for that. I spent a good deal of time as she grew older making it up to her. Thankfully, I never lost sight of the life she envisioned for me. That helped to bring me back when I strayed. It was a combination of her vision and my choices. In addition, it involved a spiritual perspective from the God to whom she introduced me.

Which Way?

I recall a "Rest of the Story" account by the master story-teller Paul Harvey. He told of two brothers. One became a physician and the other was serving most of his life in prison. Interviewed individually, the defining question that was asked was "To what in your life would you attribute your motivation to turn out the way you have?" The physician answered, "How could I have turned out any different with the parents I had?" The stunning conclusion to this entire account, was that the brother in prison gave exactly the same answer.

I suppose someone might conclude that the parents favored one child over the other. That was certainly the case with Jacob and Esau. The father and mother of those boys were not on the same page. In the long run, we learn more about forgiveness and peacemaking from this story, than about child rearing. I have observed over the years that some children turn out to be stellar adults, even though their parents kept their own agendas without much attention given to nurturing their children. I also have witnessed broken hearts in parents, who have poured themselves into their children, only to see them go in directions they never envisioned. There are many parents with broken hearts in this respect.

One of our favorite nurses took loving care of Brenda during her cancer treatment. Her care comes with a lot of hugs and sometimes the words "I love you." I get the impression that this nurse would be gentle in any profession she chose. Somehow, she would find a way to be a gentle mechanic and (I promise) I would take my vehicles to her.

Once she told us that all through her education, her father thought she was studying to be a doctor. When she completed her training and showed him her diploma, he cried. What do we do to our kids? Many dads have done a terrible job encouraging their kids. For years, I have worked with people who have chosen a life below their capabilities. I cannot count the number of times I heard "Nothing I ever did made my dad happy." The story of the nurse has a happy ending. Her dad finally came to grips with her choice of a career and is proud.

A parent who calls things as they are, must be admired. What parent would not be proud to have a son win a top award in sports? However, this young man has had challenges staying out of trouble—even with the law. A recent headline quotes the father: "I hate to say it, but I hope he goes to jail." This young man's life has not turned out as the father envisioned. It takes a lot of love for a father to make a statement like that. However, his son still has time.

Another Hurt (Loneliness?)

I conducted a graveside service for a 64-year-old man. He had one brother and two sons. The brother and one son came. Attendance was very small, less than 20, including a few grandchildren and other relatives. The only emotion I witnessed was from the brother. There are countless experiences such as this, where years of damage was done during the life of the individual. It often is a time of coming together but sometimes not. One situation I recall produced no one at all. This individual was committed to his final resting place by four people: the funeral director, two grave diggers and me. At least the cemetery workers had enough respect to remove their caps and stand by the grave before finishing their job. I made it a point to thank them.

I conducted a funeral service for a young man in his 30's. The dad and his wife (not the mother of his children) were visiting with me. It was a decent size crowd. The dad pointed out his daughter, visiting with others in attendance. He told me that today was the first time she had spoken to him in sixteen years. This family already had a painful situation to face. They were now faced with the task of dealing with a strained relationship that had festered for years. With the silence broken between father and daughter, hope seemed possible. It certainly yielded an opportunity for a few remarks in the eulogy, regarding the value of family.

How can families gain strength from one another in the midst of extreme pain? How can anyone face and survive an abrupt change in the family structure, with the limited resources they have from living a life unthreatened by hardship and challenges? Life was not intended to be a continual trip to

Disney World. Paul Harvey would say: "You can run, but you can't hide." It is difficult enough, for those who have a spiritual perspective for their lives.

Loss of A Child

I am convinced that when death takes a child from a parent, it creates a special kind of pain, regardless of the child's age. My brother's life ended on his forty-second birthday. My parents were both alive to deal with it. At the visitation the night before the funeral, I saw my dad cry for the first time in my life. He was 65.

Not long ago, I conducted a funeral for a man in his 40's. The family asked for me, because I had conducted the service for their father two years earlier. I typically visit and pray with the family prior to the service. I witnessed the face of a mother, whose heart was filled with pain.

I've already told of our grandson who stopped breathing in his crib, just short of three months of age. Just a few days ago, with a police officer, I entered the emergency room of the children's hospital, when the officer was dispatched to an incident involving a patient there. Parking outside the door and walking through the corridor proved to be very difficult for me. It was the same facility where we received the news of our grandson's death. Although years had passed, the words of the ER doctor still haunt me: "The baby is dead." Our family has been given many blessings to offset the pain of that night. However, there still is a brain cell or two in my head, that retains the memory of something happening that was entirely unexpected.

I was at the cemetery recently with my younger sister. She keeps the flowers fresh on the grave of her husband. It has been years, but the connection still is there. What captures me most about this, is the parents of my brother-in-law (whose earthly remains rest next to their youngest son) experienced the death of all three of their children in their own lifetimes. The oldest son lost his life in an auto accident. The only daughter lost her battle with cancer, just a few months before my brother-in-law experienced a horrible industrial accident that took his life. The parents lived several more years. When my last parent died, it occurred to me that I now was an orphan. Is there a word that describes a couple who has witnessed all their children enter eternity? During the remaining years of their lives, I do not recall a day that I didn't wonder how a mom and dad make it to the end of their own lives with this tremendous emptiness. It must have taken a special effort on their part. Trite words of encouragement would come up short.

I am an enabler by nature. I take on the pain of those in whom I have invested. As longevity sneaks up on me, I am learning to live in a new way. No one loves their grandchildren more than Brenda and me. Issues with one have placed a special burden on our hearts and have had a significant effect on our emotions. A conversation with a dear friend at the beginning of this latest crisis brought this comment: "You have seven grandchildren. Don't be so torn down by issues with one that you have nothing left to give the other six." Those words are in my head on a daily basis. It is not fair to the rest of the family, to deplete my effectiveness on their behalf.

Loneliness, disappointment and separation are part of a broken world. It is tempting to question our own effectiveness and assume guilt for the failures. If I reach out with my heart to the lonely, disappointed and grieving and see little (if any) response to my efforts, what have I done wrong?

I see so much of myself in this passage from R.W. Long's book *Push the Rock*, "For most of my life I have felt like I'm spiritually deficient when it comes to understanding whatever it is that God wants me to do. I often think of myself as a spiritual Forrest Gump. As a Christian, I envy those who say that God speaks clearly to them. On many occasions, I have wished God would send an e-mail, or a Facebook message, or a Tweet, or a text message, or even a telegram telling me what it is I am to do. Whatever it is, I'll do it because it is my earnest desire."

In Matthew 28 we find Jesus issuing the great commission to some doubting disciples: "Then the eleven disciples went to Galilee, to the mountain where Jesus had told them to go. When they saw him, they worshipped him, but some doubted." Three times, Peter (the rock) denied that he even knew Jesus. Judas betrayed Him. He spent three and a half years training a handful of men to carry on His work when He left. Often it appeared that His efforts were producing no results at all. Neither did He escape hurt and disappointment. But Jesus looked past the moment. It's a good thing for us that He did.

Chapter 17

Where is Dad?

"So you will walk in the way of good men and keep to the paths of the righteous." —Proverbs 2:20

Where is Dad?

I raised that question at a meeting with other pastors. What is the reaction of parents, when they learn of the destructive behavior of one of their children? One pastor answered, "They don't care."

I am not certain I can accept that. Listening to parents pour out their hearts when they learn of a child hurting someone else, leads me to think differently. There is a temptation to feel a little responsible and wonder where we went wrong. What did I fail to teach them? Did they witness something in me, that would lead them to conclude it was acceptable to take advantage of someone else for my own benefit? We would like to know that we instilled better values in them.

Prayer Requests from Young Offenders

Often a chaplain shares a list of prayer requests from young people in juvenile detention. These offenders are teenagers and younger. Spiritual issues have not dominated their thinking. Their lives have been in turmoil, due to dysfunctional families, inappropriate companions and other reasons that are a mystery to most. They are now facing the legal system, probation, and perhaps extended incarceration.

The chaplain offers them the opportunity to express prayer requests for their lives and the results are often stunning:

- Pray that me and my mom's relationship falls back into place and gets stronger.

- Can you pray that I go home and become somebody in life and make people happy and change me?

- Pray that when I go to court, that whatever judge I get shows mercy and lets me go home or can you ask God to proceed in a miracle because I need to go home for my momma's health.

- Pray that me and my mom's relationship gets better, and we start talking again.

- Pray for everyone around me, my enemies, family and friends.

- Please pray for me to gain control of my anger and violence.

- Pray that I can keep from being discouraged from getting locked up again.

- Pray for my mom, who has cancer.

- Pray for my little daughter and for the family who is taking care of her.

- Pray for me to go to school when I get out of here and stay at home and not do any drugs.

- Pray for my momma's health and that when I go to court, whatever is best for me happens.

- Please pray that the judge picks a good place for me to go.

These requests are sent out to supporters. I read them all. Many of them contain the warm thoughts of mothers. I cannot recall ever reading a heartfelt mention of the father. Many dads have checked out of the lives of their children. This is a crucial age for these young people. They are looking for tools to negotiate life and Dad is not there. He has his own agenda and the kids suffer for lack of direction. It is only in rare instances, that mom can do it alone.

A report was done on the occupants of death row; the number of these prisoners, who had no relationship with their fathers was absolutely stunning.

I was along on a police call, where a fourteen-year-old girl walked out of the house and the mother could not find her. This was a special needs girl with autism and depression. Mom was raising her and two other children alone. She seemed to interact with the other two children very well. They retrieved her chair to use outdoors and a jacket to keep her warm. They were very respectful. It just seemed obvious that this mother was dealing with these kids, without their father. It is not uncommon.

Isn't this interesting? "Fathers do not aggravate your children, or they will become discouraged." (Colossians 2:21) "Fathers do not provoke your children to anger by the way you treat them. Rather, bring them up with the discipline and instruction that comes from the Lord." (Ephesians 6:4) Notice how both passages stress the function of fathers.

Most of the police calls I experience that involve misbehavior of an older child, are placed by the mother. When we arrive, I sometimes ask where the father is. Many of these calls would never occur, if there were a father in the home (not a stepfather, grandfather, uncle or boyfriend). No one can fully replace a father in the life of a child he took part in bringing into the world.

The family courts are full of child support cases. The father had a part in this child being here, but many are seldom willing to pay child support. Ask any dad who has remained in a home with the mother and built their relationship over time. They will acknowledge that they paid more "child support," than any father who was sanctioned by the court to do so. We also earned the right to be a part of their growing up. I never have met a dad who did it perfectly. Being there and loving their mother counts for a lot.

On one police call, the youngest son was unruly and physical with some of the members of the family. The young man had violated his most recent probation. He had been in trouble numerous times, yet his father continued to drain his own finances to rescue him. I asked his older sister (who made the call to 911, after being strangled by her brother): "Where is Dad?"

"He is in the house and won't come out." I then asked, "What will Dad do now that he has violated his probation?" She replied, "He can't do anything, he's used all of his money." I spoke with the mother, but the father was completely depleted over his son's behavior.

How Far Can You Steer a Child?

I can't count the number of times I have had the opportunity to talk with a parent (usually the mother) following an incident with the child. I was stunned when two children (eight and six) became abusive with their mother, because she kept their cell phones as discipline. I asked her the same question I have asked many mothers, both single and married. "Is the dad anywhere around?" I usually know the answer before I ask. He has abandoned the family or has his own agenda. His help is not available.

Brenda and I attended a dinner that honored donors to a non-profit organization. I was a board member. The organization worked with dads, who were delinquent with child support, to turn their hearts toward their children, regardless of the relationship with the mother. This organization provides a chaplain in the civil courts, where about 1,000 divorces are granted each month. In some cases (through counseling), marriages are saved after they reevaluate their priorities. There are also two chaplains in the juvenile detention center. These good people have time with each inmate and do an enormous amount of good to give these offenders new criteria for making choices each day.

At the dinner, Brenda and I sat next to the juvenile judge, who was the featured speaker for the evening. I asked the judge, "Can you pinpoint the main cause for the lack of direction of our young people today?" The honorable judge didn't even pause to think about the answer: "The lack of a father figure in the home." That has motivated me to ask the question so often, when an officer and I deal with the adverse behavior of a young person. We typically receive the call from the mother, who is experiencing "out of control" behavior from her child.

Do Both Parents Really Matter?

A home is just not complete with one parent missing. It also is not functioning well, when the mother allows abuse from the man in the house. Children witness this and draw conclusions, as to their role in relationships.

There are startling statistics regarding the presence of an involved father in the life of their children. These figures come from the National Center for Fathering.

Children who are raised in a home with an involved father are:

- 39% more likely to earn mostly A's in school
- 45% less likely to repeat a grade
- 60% less likely to be suspended/expelled from school
- Two times more likely to attend college and find stable employment
- 75% less likely to have a teen birth
- 80% less likely to spend time in jail

In his book, *The Good Dad,* Jim Daly cited United States Census figures. It is reported that fifteen million kids live apart from their biological fathers. This represents one out of every three American children.

He adds that the stats are no better for girls. "They, too, struggle as kids and into adulthood. Moreover, females raised without fathers are four times more likely to engage in sexual intercourse at an early age, and more than twice as likely to get pregnant early." These figures are documented in their report "Fathering in America," May 2009.

I read a story described as Dad's Message, about doing things for his ex-wife. The dad wrote "It's my ex-wife's birthday today, so I got up early and brought flowers and cards and a gift over for the kids to give her and helped them make her breakfast. I'm raising two little men. The example I set for how I treat their mom, is going to significantly shape how they see and treat women and affect their perception of relationships."

Proverbs 23 is full of wisdom for relationships. In verse 24, we read "The father of a righteous child has great joy; a man who fathers a wise son rejoices in him. May your father and mother rejoice; may she who gave you birth be joyful!" I have a clear vision of the time I sat too long in a left turn lane, after the light had turned green. The man in the pickup made significant use of his horn, then drove beside me and presented me with a vulgar hand signal with a finger extended. His young son, in the passenger seat, looked at me through the closed window and stuck out his tongue. I made a mistake—I admit it. It troubled me to see a young boy learn such a negative response, from the man who is most important in his life.

When our adult son was in elementary school, I asked his principal for her estimate of the number of students in her school who lived in a fatherless home. She quickly responded with at least 40%. That nearly knocked me out of my chair. I was raised in that kind of home.

As a young child, my dad was gone a great deal with his own agenda. He was often derelict of the family finances, certainly inattentive to me, and he left completely, when I turned fourteen. I found him four years later in California, when I was stationed with the Navy.

I shudder to think where I would be today, had Mother not put me around good families. Once I attempted to serve in an organization called Big Brothers. I was literally smothered by young boys starving for a male influence in their lives. It took away from my own family and I was not very good at balancing my time back then.

Years later, I served as a board member for the nonprofit already mentioned. My specific area of interest was being one of the teachers in a class of fathers who were delinquent in child support. After the ten-week class, I was amazed (and still am) at the effect this time had in connecting those dads with their children, even though the relationship between the parents had deteriorated. This demonstrates that even though a couple's relationship might deteriorate, a dad can make a conscious commitment to fulfill the purpose in the life of his children, only he can fulfill.

Parental Expectations

In a graduate school counseling class, we utilized triads, a group of three students who spent some designated class time in "counseling" sessions. One person would bring a challenge or struggle to class and the other two would listen and help the troubled person come to grips with a solution. My triad consisted of myself, another male student and a lady whose husband was a medical student. One day she came to our triad totally wiped out emotionally. Her husband's best friend (also a medical student) had committed suicide.

We encouraged her to talk. This young man had pressure from his father to become a doctor. The only problem with this, was that this son clearly could see that his gifts were not consistent with his father's wish. He sought to satisfy his father by becoming a medical student, rather than tell his father he was not interested in making medicine his career. Instead, he chose a permanent escape. Her husband was devastated.

I have a friend whose only son completed medical school, only to discover that he would rather work with computers. My friend accepted his son's decision and did nothing to make him feel guilty for turning down, what many would consider a great opportunity.

In an interview, Duke Ellington was asked about those difficult early days most musicians have. The Duke said, "I didn't have any." "You didn't starve or suffer?" the interviewer asked. Mr. Ellington responded, "No, I started right out doing what I most liked to do, working with music. I had faith in myself and it was easy. When I was a little boy, I was loved so much I don't think my feet hit the ground, until I was seven years old."

One of the most gifted pianists and composers of the modern world played at two events attended by Brenda and me. Then Brenda took our girls to a local concert and (afterward) captured him exiting the stage door for a group photo. The music world would be missing something significant today without his contribution. His performances left a person spellbound and brought tears to my eyes. His gift was one that was obvious at a very young age.

Once I read an account of a conversation (told by the man himself) between this maestro and his father. They were discussing the work of Mozart. The conversation drifted to the fact that Mozart composed a symphony at the age of 8. The dad asked his child "where is YOUR symphony?" We have discussed instances of an absent or uninvolved father. There is another extreme as well. Paul wrote it at least two ways: "Fathers, do not provoke your children to anger" (Ephesians 6:4), and "Fathers, do not provoke your children, so they will not become discouraged" (Colossians 3:21). I have spent my years of fatherhood examining disparaging remarks to my own children. This effort has produced some apologies over the years — from me.

Can you imagine being the son/daughter of the Pharisee, who came to the temple and prayed next to the Publican? He compared himself to the Publican as he prayed and offered thanks to God that he was not like the other guy. He envisioned himself better than the other person. It is unreasonable to expect our children to be what WE want them to be. The passage in Proverbs addresses our responsibility to train up a child, according to his "natural bent." Proverbs 22:6. That takes insight by us parents. When they make decisions that are destructive to their lives, it has a tendency to bring us to our knees.

Thumbing through the history of the church in which I grew up, I was reminded of the early days of this great place. Soon after my family moved from Nashville (I was seven months old), this church had its beginning. The first meetings were held in a vacant building, near where the new building was being built. I have childhood memories of sitting on sawhorses next to my mother, sister and brother during church services.

The second minister to preside had a son my age and we went all through school together. It was common for me to visit their home, spend the night and eat meals at the family table. I experienced a far different version of family life there, than at my own home. My mother was a good woman. Sister and Brother loved me, and Little Sister was my buddy. However, we just did not have a dad to give us the leadership and direction that needs to come from the head of the family.

Father Figures Are Within Reach

My last year or so in the military was spent questioning the value of faith in God. I made a call to Yokohama. I wanted to visit with the chaplain. I was confused. I didn't feel ready to return to the States and civilian life. I called this chaplain to say farewell and resolve my spiritual confusion. I told him I would be willing to drive to his office for a visit. He asked if we could do it over the phone. That didn't help.

When I returned to Texas, I asked my hero minister if I could visit with him regarding my doubts. As we visited, he treated me like I was the only person in the world. He prayed with me and arranged several meetings for me with a wise elder. To this day, I place this experience as one of the defining times of my life. This elder listened intently to my heart, talked with me and lifted me up in prayer.

From those meetings, I learned some things:

1. It is appropriate for a man to have a strong faith in God and confidence in His presence.

2. It is appropriate for a man to listen to the heart of another person.

3. It is appropriate for a man to possess and project a gentle spirit.

Upon my discharge from the Navy, one of my mother's friends took me to a local golf course and taught me how to swing a club. I learned to love the game. I still am not very good, but I love to play. It became an excuse to spend time with someone, when golf was not the most important reason for being together.

It lifted me up, when my minister invited me to play golf with him every Monday. Isn't Monday traditionally a day off for preachers and barbers? It added to the day to have the church choir director play along as well. This man had one of the most beautiful baritone voices I ever have heard. He often took me with him when he sang at events—even rehearsals. My dad took me to a few car races and a couple of air shows. Those were meaningful but not one word about God or being a good man.

Thumbing through the church history book recently, I read handwritten notes from the first two ministers, who served during my years of maturing. The one who served as my minister the longest, concluded his remarks with *you are my friend.* When I read that, it melted my heart even years after it was written. This good man and his wife are with the Lord now, along with their oldest son, with whom I was closely connected growing up. The memory of this family occupies a significant part of my heart and is a large part of the man I am today.

I became a bit of an outcast to my dad, when I became a minister. It was a slap in his face. He resented the church. As a child, I recall Mother loading my sister and me in the car one Sunday morning for the drive to church. Dad was so angry that his children were being exposed to something he hated, that he grabbed the left front fender of the 1946 Pontiac with his bare hands and completely ripped it off. What a vision for young eyes. I am glad I didn't follow his example or pattern my priorities after his.

There are doctors whose sons became doctors and there are ministers whose sons followed in the footsteps of their fathers. I would be totally blown away. Humility might be difficult. I am afraid I would give myself more credit as a parent, than I deserve. I have a difficult enough time walking in the steps of Jesus. We have three good children, and each has made me proud. Certainly, they are not perfect, but neither am I.

It was her first Father's Day without him. She walked by and I couldn't help but speak to her. Her dad's passing was still fresh. Since I knew him longer than she had been in the world, I assured her that the family was being thought of. I don't recall the words exactly, but it was something like this: "We dads want you to miss us being there. But it is most important to us that we set a good example for you to follow through life." I didn't learn that from a book.

It came from living, being a dad and knowing what I missed. It also came from being around good men, who took a genuine interest in me.

I have heard it said that a person cannot give to another what he does not have. It would have been a real bonus to see that gentleness coming from the right person—my own father. However, if Proverbs 2:20 carries any weight at all, it is fine to receive this influence from someone we respect and who takes an interest in us. Thank God for them.

Chapter 18

Explaining the Unexplainable

"Don't be afraid. Just stand still and watch the Lord rescue you today…The Lord himself will fight for you." —Exodus 14:13-14

My life has consisted of many unexplainable experiences. I would guess that yours has as well.

I don't remember much about that night, sometime in 1960. Neither my friend nor I went many places alone. Dave and I joined the Navy together in September 1959. We were sent to basic training in San Diego, came home on leave together, then both of us were assigned to the USS Princeton, an aircraft carrier harbored in Long Beach, California. The ship sailed the Far East beginning in February, then returned in August. We did most everything together. However, not this time and I don't recall why.

I left the ship and went someplace in Los Angeles. It was a club where they played music I liked. I was too young to drink alcohol, so that was out. I do recall striking up a conversation with a civilian gentleman. We both liked the same kind of music. We talked a lot about what was going on in our lives.

The guy offered me a ride back to the ship. It was late, and I needed to get back. As we walked together around to the back of the building, I was surprised when he began hitting me in the head with his fists, knocking me to the ground. No one else was close and I lay there, as if I were unconscious. I did not know what kind of damage he could do, beyond what he already had done. He began looking for anything valuable I might be carrying. The first thing he took from me was my watch. I still grieve about that. It was a gift from my mother, when I graduated from high school. I recall him looking in my rear pocket, asking where my wallet was. I was wearing my white Navy uniform that night and the pants had a flap on the front with thirteen buttons (representing the original thirteen colonies). I learned from older sailors to carry my wallet hooked over the top of that flap leaving those top buttons undone. It was the only place for a wallet, but my attacker didn't know that.

He gave up looking and walked away. I lay there for a few minutes, making certain he had left. Then I went back inside the building and called a cab to take me back to the ship.

That was the only time in my life that I was a victim of someone's violence. I have wondered through the years what happened to that fellow. Was this the beginning or continuation of a life of crime for him? He wasn't that old (maybe mid-twenties). I have wondered about anyone else he may have victimized. It also has occurred to me the extreme emotional pain his parents might have felt, if they ever learned of his destructive behavior. Surely, they envisioned a better life for him.

It also occurred to me through the years that I survived something that night that many have not. It is a horrible memory, and this is the only accounting I have given since it happened. I cannot rewrite my life story and exclude this experience. Neither can I explain why I survived, when many good people have not. I do not hold to the view that God turns His back on some people and rescues others. I know that Elijah searched for God in a whirlwind but found Him in a whisper. Jacob found Him in his dreams, Moses in a burning bush. The writer of Hebrews encourages us to "not neglect to show hospitality to strangers, for by so doing some people have shown hospitality to angels without knowing it." (Hebrews 13:2)

Stranger in L.A.

I had disembarked a military transport plane after a 36-hour ride from Japan, where I had spent two years. A bus took me to an area of L.A. I knew very little about this city. My goal was to walk a few blocks and catch another bus to my friend's house in Pacoima. It was the middle of the night. I had no idea where I was, and I was carrying a large heavy Samsonite suitcase. The Navy uniform gave me away. A block or so from my destination, I was so exhausted that I was practically dragging my suitcase. A sizable gentleman walked up beside me and said, "Let me help." He picked up the Samsonite and carried it across a busy street, sat it on the sidewalk a few feet from my destination and left before I could even thank him. Where he came from has been a mystery to me since 1962. This experience helped compensate for my previous L.A. experience. It was a generous gesture and couldn't have come at a better time.

Paris

Brenda and I had been in London on a company trip. One of her life dreams was to visit Switzerland. I had made friends with a gentleman who had been to Zermatt, Switzerland many times. He knew a lady in that city who owned a hotel. We made arrangements to go there from London. We took far too much luggage. There were more bags than we could carry comfortably and we had a long way to go. (We pack better today.) We flew from Heathrow airport across the English Channel and landed at De Galle Airport in Paris. In the days before cell phones, the only way we could call home was a phone booth at the airport. We headed straight for it. We both missed our children, we were halfway around the world from them and we had another week to go. After the call and tears, we dragged our luggage to the subway entry across the street. We knew where we were going. However, we had no idea how to get there. Going down the long ramp toward the subway, a nice gentleman (not even a Frenchman) stopped and asked us where we were going. After we told him, he pointed us to the proper subway and gave clear directions. The man then reached into his pocket and pulled out more than enough French currency to pay our fare. All we had was U.S. dollars and pounds from England. This amazing dream come true was made even more amazing, by the unidentified gentleman whose kindness was totally unexpected.

After spending six glorious days at the base of the Matterhorn, we wondered (and still do) who that nice man was that came to our rescue in Paris.

Who Handed Me That Money?

With the encouragement of a supporting church in Tennessee and a group of new Christians in northwestern Wisconsin, we made a move to serve the new church there. With no working fund and no personal assets, it was a significant mystery how our family would find a place to live, much less contribute to an infant church.

Staying with one family after another, didn't provide much stability. Once we stayed with a single lady who was taking care of her elderly mom. Two story homes were foreign to us and our daughter fell all the way down the stairs of the farmhouse. Totally dependent on other people, I chastised myself, since I take 1 Timothy 5:8 very seriously, "Anyone who does not provide for their relatives, and especially for their own household, has denied the faith and is worse than an unbeliever." It was my job to provide for my family and I was not doing it very well.

We began looking for a house to buy. The chances of doing so seemed slim, since we had nothing for a down payment. At a reception for the "new family from Texas," a gentleman walked up to me and put a significant amount of money into my hand. It was around the first part of September, so maybe he was looking for a tax deduction. He explained that the money was to help secure a home for my family. We found a house that was built in 1890 and did some upgrades with the help of another member. The generous man and his wife were not among the most active members of the church. When we moved three years later to another part of the state, we never heard from them again. To this day, it is a mystery what motivated a fellow church member to hand me that much cash. He put no conditions on the use of the money and made it clear that he didn't expect repayment.

An Accepted Offer

I was driving in the area where we would be working and making our home. Staying with another family was becoming more awkward. We were very anxious to have our own home.

I drove by a cute old house on an acre and a half. This two-story house was built in the late 1800s and had a detached garage. There was a "for sale" sign in the front yard. I saw someone there, so I stopped, thinking it might be the real estate agent. It was the owner. We talked, and I asked him the price, $21,000. I asked him what he would be willing to take. He said $15,000. We exchanged contact information. I was certain that we could handle that price, especially since we had good credit and cash for a down payment. He accepted my lower price, which I soon learned through a call from an angry real estate agent.

Reduced Rent?

My last preaching job lasted seven months. That job was the way I supported my family. While employed, we lived in a home owned by the church. It was now necessary to vacate that home—quickly. It was obvious that my family had no place to live and I had no way of making a living. I had spent some time in insurance sales, but it never was a full-time occupation. The director of the school I attended for theology training made a personal referral (along with a phone call) to a church in Louisiana. The church had me come over for two Sundays to preach for them and meet everyone. I went alone. Brenda did not want to travel. I was offered the job. I came home and told her. She replied that she and the children had talked and didn't want to move again. I had a dilemma. (One seminary gives the following explanation to the students: If you are called to a work and your wife is not, then you haven't been called to that work). It was necessary for me to reject the job offer.

I needed to support my family. However, I didn't have a way to do that, even though I had a master's degree and twelve years of experience as a minister. I entered the insurance field with less than 100% enthusiasm. The gentleman to whom I was assigned, had almost an identical history as mine. He had achieved considerable success in business and still worked in ministry.

At a coffee shop one morning, he asked me if I was going to work at the insurance profession or continue looking for a preaching job. After several minutes of silence, I picked insurance as a career choice: "If you can do it, I can do it." That was not a statement of condescension. Knowing his story convinced me it was possible.

We needed a place to live. We found a house in the same area, where we already lived. The owner listened to our situation. He was asking $500 rent for his house. For some unknown reason (I still don't know why), he told us he would charge us $300 a month for the first six months and then raise it to $500. That relieved a great deal of pressure.

Where Did He Come From?

We were on a Mediterranean cruise with a group of people from church. This has been a dream of mine since age 17. Near the end of Navy basic training, we were handed a questionnaire asking our preference for duty. A friend from home had been sent to the Mediterranean Sea on a ship and that sounded like great duty. I put that down but was assigned to an aircraft carrier on the West Coast. After an eight-month cruise through the Far East, I received orders to Japan for two years. I'm not complaining. A lot of what and who I am, was due to that Far East experience. I still love Japan.

Brenda and I had been to Europe three times but never on a cruise. After spending the night in Venice, Italy, one of the memories we wished to create was a Venetian gondola ride. We booked it ahead but had a terrible time locating the place to catch the gondola. We found the locals very unhelpful with directions—possibly due to the language barrier.

After creating that memory, we attempted to find our way back to the train station that would take us to our hotel. We got on a water bus that took us in the wrong direction. After heading the correct way, we questioned; were we going toward or away from town? Which stop do we get off at, to go to the train station? Again—very little help.

A gentleman with his family overheard Brenda's desperation and came to our assistance. He took pity on this couple approaching their 52nd anniversary and said "Just stay with us. We are going to the same place." We were trusting (as well as desperate). It was late in Venice, and our body clocks were still on Texas time. We got off the water bus with them and followed them to the ticket kiosk at the train station. He purchased tickets for his family of five and two more for the people he had just met. We followed them on the train, got off with them, when we recognized our hotel, got to our room and crashed from exhaustion.

As it turned out, we were not only were staying at the same hotel, we all were going on the same cruise. I made sure that he had our contact information. They live in St. Louis.

Where Is Mr. Horton?

Brenda and I were asked by the mother of one of our grandsons, if we would take him into our home. She was convinced that we could provide for him, better than she was able to. We insisted on getting court documents, so we could take an active role in his life at our discretion. Soon after this was done, we sought state medical assistance (Medicaid—in some cases a dependent child living with grandparents is entitled to Medicaid, regardless of the financial situation of the grandparents). We obtained papers and sent them off. Following up, we were told they had not arrived. Several efforts were made. We either left some question unanswered, failed to provide the necessary information, or no one could locate the paperwork.

Another set of papers were completed, with the intention of hand delivering them to the headquarters. I called the office and spoke with a lady who directed us miles away from where we needed to be. I called back and someone else gave general directions but the wrong address. Once again, I placed a call which was answered by a gentleman, named Mr. Horton, who asked exactly what issues we had faced. He became frustrated that we were having issues.

Mr. Horton directed us straight to the building, with a promise to meet us by the entrance. He smelled of cigarette smoke. We followed him into the building to a cubicle. He was more than a little frustrated that we had experienced such difficulty in getting anything done. He promised to have the case transferred to him and get everything processed in a few days. He did just that.

When it came time to renew this coverage, I had a question to ask the caseworker. I called the extension we had been using for Mr. Horton and someone different answered the phone. The lady explained that she was our caseworker and the gentleman I asked for was unknown to her or anyone in her office. Every six months, the renewal continued smoothly (even with a different caseworker). We followed the procedures established by the mysterious gentleman who helped. Renewing the coverage each time was routine and the grandson was cared for under the program, until he turned 19.

We had prayed for years that we might have a more active role in the life of this grandson. God brought that about as well. There were heartaches and challenges along the way and we still carry some of those today. God has been faithful in every challenge. People and/or means He has provided, have opened doors that would not have been opened otherwise.

Grace We Don't Deserve

Psalms, Chapter 107 is another narrative of the history of God's people told centuries after it happened. It was an account that the Israelites have heard all their lives. The writer concludes "…those who are wise will take all this to heart; they will see in our history the faithful love of the Lord." It is obvious to anyone that God never provided protection, security, and guidance because His people were obedient. They rebelled many times and Moses stepped in to defend them. God was certainly capable of wiping out the entire nation and starting over. We don't deserve it either.

Think back on your life. How many near misses can you recall? How many unexplained victories? God can rescue a prostitute and place her in the family tree of Jesus Christ. He can cause a young boy to defeat an enemy giant with a sling and one stone (notice that he had five stones just in case). He can open the doors of a prison, so His servants can carry on their work. He can bring about reconciliation between two brothers who had every reason to be alienated for life. He can turn His back on His only son, as he hung on the cross for the sins of unworthy humans. There is significant value in remembering.

Chapter 19

Pain

*"One of the men lying there had been sick for thirty-eight years.
When Jesus saw him and knew he had been ill for a long time, he asked
him, 'would you like to get well?'"* —John 5:5-6

When we face sickness or injury, we want to be made well. Why?

If we are made well, what will we do with the days we are given when our health returns? How will we use the time? Will we plop down in front of the television? Will we walk around wearing headphones for entertainment? Play more golf? Travel the world? Is that all there is to a healthy and fulfilling life?

I shared a burning personal question with several people. However, I did not receive a meaningful response. It was no fault of theirs. I am also having trouble providing an answer. Here is my dilemma: I have been one of the healthiest people that I have known for my age. All my doctor visits yielded no real issues. That is significant, since the news from my high school class frequently reports that another classmate has passed. The list just keeps getting longer. I now have outlived my dad. However, toward the end of his life he was confined to a nursing home following a serious stroke, drawn up in a fetal position, couldn't speak and lived only three additional months.

The recent words of my doctor were "This is not good." I've never heard those words, with regard to my health. An EKG determined that I had atrial fibrillation. I was prescribed blood thinners, in preparation for a procedure known as a cardioversion. I was admitted to the hospital as an outpatient with family and friends around me. I was told the doctor had four cardioversions scheduled for that same day. Routine for him perhaps, but not me.

I hadn't experienced the prick of IV needles in years. Paddles lay beside the bed ready to be placed on my chest and back. While under anesthesia, my heart was administered a shock at the right moment to return it to a normal rhythm. It worked—for a while. I continue to take blood thinners (probably for the rest of my life) and am under the care of a cardiologist. Eight months later, there was surgery for an inguinal hernia. I am stunned. Why did I start running 45 years ago and fill my life with cardio exercises?

A CT scan to evaluate my hernia revealed much more. A total of six defects were revealed, ranging from cysts on my liver, issues with my sigmoid colon along with an enlarged prostate, heart and spleen. I wondered if this was the beginning of the end.

I have been confronted with my own mortality. So far, I have outlived every male in my family, except for a cousin in California. I was honored to conduct his memorial service when illness took him at age 86. There has been a great deal of introspection about how I have used the time I have had so far. I conducted a graveside service for an 84-year-old lady. She had not achieved greatness in the manner the world often defines greatness. She did not build a business or earn a college degree. It was moving to hear her six children share heartwarming memories of her sewing their clothes and making clothes for their Barbie dolls. Her husband had been married to this good lady for 63 years and still was deeply in love with her.

Getting Much More Than We Ask For

This brings to mind two incidents from the Bible. One was of King Solomon being offered a wish by God himself. Solomon (at that time) had the desire to be a good king. He simply asked for wisdom. God responded by not only giving him wisdom but fame and wealth. God gave Solomon a great deal more than he asked for.

This 92-year-old gentleman was happy to get a wife 63 years ago.

According to what he told me, he got much more than expected. He went on and on about the virtues of this woman, that were not obvious to him when they married. The children related much more. How many of us have seen God do that for us? We find a partner and have children. In the beginning, there is not even a glimpse of everything that is in store for us over the next several years.

The other account is that of King Hezekiah. This is found in 2 Kings 20. About that time, Hezekiah became deathly ill, and the prophet Isaiah was sent to visit him. He gave the king this message: "'This is what the Lord says: Set your affairs in order, for you are going to die. You will not recover from this illness.'

When Hezekiah heard this, he turned his face to the wall and prayed to the Lord, 'remember, O Lord, how I have always been faithful to you and have served you single-mindedly, always doing what pleases you.' Then he broke down and wept bitterly. However, before Isaiah had left the middle courtyard, this message came to him from the Lord: 'Go back to Hezekiah, the leader of my people. Tell him 'This is what the Lord, the God of your ancestor David, says: I have heard your prayer and seen your tears. I will heal you, and three days from now, you will get out of bed and go to the Temple of the Lord. I will add fifteen years to your life, and I will rescue you and this city from the king of Assyria. I will defend this city for my own honor and for the sake of my servant David.'"

First, dying at this time was not in Hezekiah's plan. He had things going on in his life. Second, God can take what appears to be a terminal situation and turn it around. Third, God just may have His own agenda in granting these additional years and Hezekiah fit into this plan.

Our Plans vs God's Plans

We live with a false sense of control over life. When we flip a light switch, we expect the room to light up. We turn the key to our car and we expect the car to start. We expect hot water to come from the faucet, when we turn the left handle. What if it doesn't? What if we check the water heater, see that it is dripping and notice the flame on the burner has been extinguished. The family is not happy. Been there, done that. Going without hot water is a serious inconvenience—especially with a large family.

The plumber arrives with a new device. He informs me that it will be necessary to rebuild the platform, because this heater is a different size than the old one. I am responsible for letting the family know the water needs to be turned off for a while. This is not a terminal situation. However, it certainly puts us out of our comfort zone for a few hours.

That is what sickness does. It has a way of changing our plans. Suicide remains the number one cause of death in America. Every day in the United States, 300 females take their own lives. There is an increase in suicides or attempted suicides around the holiday season. Many have reached that level of despair in their lives and want it to end.

In most cases, we will react to a change in our physical condition. When we have a serious chest pain, pain in the arm, severe headache or other alarming symptom, we react. We educate ourselves on symptoms of various conditions and watch closely for them. When something gets our attention, we seek medical help. We fear dealing with any kind of serious illness.

In Dr. John Schnider's book *How to Live 365 Days a Year,* (2002), he reports that over 60% of those who see a doctor are there for a real illness brought on by the emotions. He referred to the condition as EII (Emotionally Induced Illness). I was intrigued by his discovery and the courage it took to talk about it.

The scriptures declare, "A happy heart makes the face cheerful." (Proverbs 15:13) If this is true, then the converse would be true. I was teaching a Sunday School class and brought this out in our discussion. One of the students was a medical doctor. I simply looked at the good doctor and asked if he would concur with Dr. Schnider's conclusion? His immediate answer was an emphatic "Yes."

There is little question that the spirit of a person's response to emotional stress affects physical health. A counselor friend assured me that in such cases, there are real symptoms. We took our son Paul to the emergency room, when he was in elementary school. His symptoms made us think it was appendicitis, as did the doctors—initially. After keeping him overnight, the doctor explained that there was nothing wrong with his appendix. We discovered that the previous day, he was called on to play the part of a character in a story the class was reading. Paul was extremely afraid and opposed to being in front of the class. His appendix (according to the doctor) was his "target organ" and reacted in such a way, that it caused real pain. It is interesting that as a young adult, Paul's appendix was removed—the only one in the family to do so.

For years, my back would hurt in response to stress. There would be so much pain in my lower back, that I found myself sliding out of the chair and crawling across the floor of our home to get around. I had an office next to a chiropractor and saw him a couple of times for adjustments in my back and neck. He told me that a common problem he deals with is pain in the back between the shoulder blades. It was a real problem with real symptoms. As he talked with the patient, he discovered the culprit was nearly always emotional stress. The area between the shoulder blades served as the target organ for that individual.

Do You Really Want to Get Well?

In John 5, we read about Jesus approaching the pool of Bethesda surrounded by sick people. "One of the men lying there had been sick for thirty-eight years. When Jesus saw him and knew he had been ill for a long time, he asked him, 'would you like to get well?'"

What kind of question is that? The man had been incapacitated for much of his life. He had come to a place where it was believed healing could occur, yet it had not happened for this man.

Do you get the urge to look at Jesus, cock your head and say, "Duh"? Who wants to be sick and stay that way?

Brenda's brother was an outpatient for a procedure by a cardiologist.

A further referral at the beginning of the next week, required him to stay in a patient room for a night or two. He remained in the outpatient area waiting for a room. None were available. Amazing isn't it? Doctors have all they can do, even with an office full of helpers. If the body malfunctions, we find a specialist who is best qualified to deal with the issue. No one likes to be sick, right? This is especially true for the number of years described in John 5.

Brenda has had two knee replacements. Each time, she was asked if she would like to have a handicap placard for her car. I confess I liked having a place to park close to the entrance at Walmart. If I cannot park close, I let her out by the door and find a parking place anywhere I can. It might cause me to walk a bit, but God blessed me with a good set of legs. For years, I ran three miles a few times a week. However, the handicap placard permitted us to park in a designated space. It took a knee replacement to earn that privilege.

I know a police officer who is sensitive to the unauthorized use of those handicap placards. He goes through parking lots and checks the validity of the sticker to see if it is on the proper vehicle. If it isn't, he intercepts the driver, confiscates the placard and issues a citation. He explained that this is an offense that has a victim. The victim is the person who really needs the parking space. This officer is very unapologetic about the citations he issues.

There is an even harsher opinion. This is not being made up. It comes from years of watching truly disabled people being deprived of assistance, because of the selfishness of someone else. Suppose a person is overweight or ill because of personal choices he/she has made. Should they be allowed permanent use of facilities and privileges made available for those who really are? My elderly sister has had cancer, knee surgery, suffers from arthritis and uses a walker. She is now confined to a wheelchair. Through the years she has refused a handicap placard. She parked a good distance from the entrance of a store. It is her opinion that she needs to walk for her health.

There are also the battery-operated carts in the store that are intended for those who need them. A person who needs one, can just cruise through the store by pushing a button. I took my mother-in-law to a store. She was definitely handicapped but there were no carts available. We sat in front on a bench waiting for someone to return a cart. When one interested employee said something, a customer got off his cart and said "You can have this one. I was just tired."

How about the attention sick people receive, while in a doctor's office or hospital? Several people take turns checking our symptoms, like we are someone special. When we are given a clean bill of health, the attention stops and we go back to the life we lived when we had no symptoms. Or do we?

Examining Priorities

I have read three books by Jess Lair, Ph.D. Dr. Lair passed away several years ago after living a full life. He explained what his life was like, prior to obtaining a Ph.D. He owned an advertising agency. He admitted he worked too much and allowed his ego to get mixed up with his possessions and lifestyle. It took a heart attack at age 35 to change his priorities. He went back to college, earned a doctorate in psychology, moved to Montana to teach in the university and wrote a few books. This provided time, attention, and stability for his family. He did not spend time regretting the past. Instead, he focused on how he could best use the present day to make a difference.

That's my kind of hero. I have made many mistakes in my life. I am not proud of some of the memories I carry around. If I dwell on them, I could grieve myself out of existence. However, a good man told me that it's partially because of the mistakes I have made in my life, that I can relate to others who are discouraged or distraught.

I am intrigued by four words Jess Lair used more than once: "I need my mistakes." James discussed the subject of wisdom. Proverbs 2 gives a long list of assets derived from wisdom. What wisdom I have, has been acquired by making mistakes. It has been a shortcut and a bonus to sit at the feet of someone who can be trusted and learn from their mistakes.

That brings me back to my unanswered question. If I am sick and desperately seeking healing, what will I do with my life, if recovery is granted? Will I go back to what I was doing before? Will I neglect the same things and people I neglected before? Will I go back to stroking my ego with inappropriate things? What would be my purpose for the reprieve I have been granted?

When King Hezekiah was told he was about to die, "he broke down and wept bitterly." (Isaiah 38:3) Isaiah was the one who broke the news to the king. After Hezekiah prayed, Isaiah was sent back to him with the news that God would grant him an additional fifteen years. Hezekiah might have had in mind how he would spend this reprieve, but God had a job for him: "I will rescue you and this city from the king of Assyria."

I confess that my life took on new meaning, when I heard my doctor say, "This is not good." The surgeon said, "That is just a bonus for living as long as you have." I was ready to call my undertaker friend to get things ready. It certainly got my attention. I have lived a long time and finally understand the value of each day of life. It has made sense for years from an intellectual point of view. It is now ingrained in my soul.

Chapter 20

What Is a Christian?

"God saved you by his grace when you believed. And you can't take credit for this, it is a gift from God. Salvation is not a reward for the good things we have done, so none of us can boast about it." —Ephesians 2:8

I agree with Jess Lair. When someone asked if he was a Christian, he would reply, "I'm working on it." It was Luke who wrote, *"When you have done everything you were told to do, you should say, we are unworthy servants; we have only done our duty"* (Luke 17:10)

I feel confident saying "I'm working on it," even though Brenda and I made a commitment through baptism over 50 years ago. So much is written about God's grace, I do not have the confidence to say I deserve any of His goodness.

My last relative on Mother's side ended his earthly walk a short time ago. He lived for 86 years. His family flew me to California to conduct his memorial service. He was a positive presence to me my entire life. I have a deep respect for the life my cousin Jim lived. Before going, I communicated at length with Jim's youngest daughter. Although I had known him longer than anyone there, his family knew him much better. She explained he had never been active in any church, but he lived his faith.

Randy Harris, in his book *Soul Work,* put it this way: "What lies behind everything I've said, is the fundamental conviction that being a follower of Jesus Christ has very little to do with going to church and a great deal to do with the transformation of our lives. And unless we start living qualitatively different lives in the world, the message that we speak has no credibility."

I've been thinking about writing my own obituary. My mother read that section of the paper every day. I am not that bad. I do glance through the list to see if there is anyone I know. Occasionally, I stop and spend a minute or two with the details. I offer a brief prayer for the families. There are some adjustments that need to be made and it is my prayer that they will find God's comfort during this difficult time.

The one fear I have, is to be known for my love for hunting, fishing, or a sports team. I didn't even purchase a college ring from my alma mater. Caring for a family was foremost.

James Dobson spoke of his mother's humor. She suggested a phrase that might be engraved on her headstone: "I told you I was sick." Mel Blanc did voices for the Disney cartoon characters—including Buggs Bunny. On his headstone in California are the words "That's all folks."

"He stretched others." How about that for a headstone? My own life has been influenced by others with large hearts. Reaching out to me, certainly earned them no financial reward. I cannot think of a single person who intentionally made a plan to put me under their wing. I was not a project to them. I observed godly character and determined it was what I wanted. Most didn't even know that they were being watched.

In my covenant group, my Christian brothers point out something that stood out to them—something I did not intentionally set out to do. It was the natural selection of behavior on my part that got their attention—not something that was done to be noticed. All the godly people throughout my life, deserve the credit. It has been the embodiment of the attitude of Jesus Christ. He is not here visibly. There are plenty of good people to watch. In fact, I would like to know that I can be one of those "good men" for someone God puts in my path.

Part of my training as a minister was to produce a commentary on 2 Corinthians. I love Chapter 5 as it discusses things that I always have been curious about. For instance, where do we go when we leave this life, what will we look like, will we have a body, will we know each other? The list goes on. In verse 6 we read "so we are always confident, even though we know that as long as we live in these bodies we are not at home with the Lord. For we live by believing and not by seeing."

I'm still working on my responsibilities as a Christian. It's worth the effort. The promises are appealing. I am also compelled to share the message, commitment, and hope with others, as I take one more ride.

Wanting to Know the Outcome Before We Begin

The world we live in, is not compatible with that concept. We like to know where we are headed, before we strike out. We like to know that results are guaranteed (or at least achievable), before we put forth the effort.

When I began to support my family in the insurance business, we submitted projections of results. Management then monitored our activity each week (sometimes each day), to see if we were on track. I lived that way for thirty years. You may have heard the business directive "begin with the end in mind." That comes from the great book *Seven Habits of Highly Effective People* by Steven Covey. This book spoke of a "Purpose Statement" and many businesses and churches developed these, as their direction declaration. Living by faith falls somewhere between "letting God do it all and trusting His guidance, as we put forth effort ourselves." Every step Brenda and I have taken, has been a step of faith. We agree. Not everything has turned out the way we had in mind, but we are experiencing far more than we ever dreamed when we began.

I receive encouragement from the Book of Hebrews, especially Chapter 11. A study of the first verse in this chapter left a lasting impression. "Faith is the confidence that what we hope for will actually happen; it gives us assurance about things we cannot see." For years, the original word translated "assurance" was found only in this verse with no presence elsewhere to compare and determine the meaning of the word. In an archeology dig, a skeleton was discovered, along with a briefcase with legal documents inside.

The skeleton turned out to be that of an attorney. He was representing a client, when Rome was confiscating real estate from citizens who could not prove ownership with appropriate documents. One document was headed with the same word translated "assurance" in the above passage. The document was a title deed supporting ownership of property by the client of the attorney. This discovery gave new meaning to the passage. Faith is the proof of ownership of the promises of God by His obedient followers. There is no wavering; no doubt that it might not be ours.

Early in our marriage, Brenda and I were in a Bible study class. The discussion was the life of Abraham. He is listed among the faithful in Hebrews 11. His entire story was not that of a spiritual giant. He lied about his relationship with Sarah and he conceived a son through Hagar, after God already had promised he would have a son with his wife. Although that was a common practice in that day, he still ignored the promise of God and that decision has affected humanity ever since.

As we sat in that Bible study, the passage was read aloud about how Sarah had respect for her husband.1 Peter 3 discusses the relationship between husband and wife. Verse 6 tells us "For instance, Sarah obeyed her husband, Abraham, and called him her master." I elbowed my wife and pointed to that verse. She slyly looked up at me and answered, "Yes, but you are not the man Abraham was." I had no response.

Through the years, though, I see myself equal to this great man in his failings. I am just as susceptible of falling short, as he ever was. I have encountered some amazing Christians in my life. None of them have been bold enough to declare that their faith is without struggle.

It is not without risk, as I already have mentioned. We met a faithful Christian couple with two children. Their world was upended, when one of them died of a recreational overdose of drugs. Sometime later, their other child lost his life in an auto accident. I was reading an account of a family who miscommunicated over the location of their young child. Each understood the other had retrieved him from the family vehicle, when in fact neither had done so. When he was discovered in a hot vehicle on a summer day, first responders could not revive him. The police officer speaking to the media stated, "This is not something that will happen to the majority of us." Yet, it happens enough around us to call our attention to situations we need to be aware of with our own children.

We can question the goodness of God or take accountability ourselves. It was "…by faith that Noah built a large boat to save his family from the flood." (Hebrews 11:7) He warned the world but only had influence over his family. "It was by faith that Abraham obeyed when God called him to leave home and go to another land that God would give him as his inheritance. He went without knowing where he was going." (Hebrews 11:8) Brenda and I have launched out in an unknown direction many times during our relationship. There was always an end in mind but not the details of the journey. Those details have worked to enrich our walk with God. That is the part that God asks us to place in His hands.

Just Keep Walking

Gideon had issues walking by faith. God referred to Gideon as a mighty warrior. He was called to deliver Israel from the hands of the Midianites. The only assurance Gideon was given was that God would be with him. Gideon still needed something more concrete. Twice, Gideon placed his infamous fleece before God, asking God for a sign that He would be with him. Gideon sought assurance by his own standards. Beginning with thirty-two thousand men, God eventually reduced that number to 300. Gideon was victorious and there was no question that victory came with the help of God. It was unorthodox. The army approached the Midianites with torches in one hand and trumpets in the other. For special effects, they smashed clay jars. This produced confusion in the Midianites and they turned on each other. This is a reminder of how God brought down the walls of Jericho. His people marched around the city seven times. After this, they shouted and blew trumpets. What kind of military strategy is that?

I identify with Gideon. More than once, I have wanted to solicit the fleece and receive assurance that my faith was pushing me in the right direction. Then I am brought back to Abraham who was directed to go to an unfamiliar place. The text simply states "…and he went without knowing where he was going." (Hebrews 11:8) He hoped against hope, became a father at age 100, and the head of a nation that established the bloodline for the birth of Jesus Christ, God's ultimate promise to the world. Abraham is truly a man who walked by faith.

I've walked with God for a long time and Brenda has walked with me. Not once did we embark on a challenge, without the assurance that God would be with us. We seldom knew the details of His presence and how it would be manifested. We prayed through each situation, never knowing what to expect. Throughout eternity, Jesus knew that his sacrifice would be significant and the human part of Him dreaded it. That is why He prayed to the Father "If you are willing, take this cup of suffering away from me. Yet I want your will to be done, not mine." (Luke 22:42) It never hurts to ask.

Gideon was a little slow to trust—but he achieved victory in a completely unorthodox manner and with far fewer resources than he originally thought he needed. He then went on to govern God's people and was unarguably better qualified for that position because of his faith experience.

In over fifty years of facing off-the-charts issues together, sometimes God got us through with far less pain than we anticipated—sometimes more. As Brenda and I reflect on them, we see God's presence in each one and we are better at the end. We have no way to envision the details of the future. It always works better when God is there.

Chapter 21

The Story of Our Lives

"Can a young woman forget her jewelry, a bride her wedding ornaments? Yet my people have forgotten me, days without number." —Jeremiah 2:3

I never have met a woman who cannot describe in detail the wedding dress she wore, regardless of how long it has been since she wore it. A 22-year-old searched for the perfect wedding gown, then she came across the gown her grandmother wore when she married her high school sweetheart in 1962. After some restoration and repair, the bride surprised her grandmother by walking into the rehearsal dinner in that special dress. It was emotional for both of them. The memories were more relevant because this grandmother had become a widow a few years before.

It is intriguing how our past affects us. There are good and bad experiences that stay with us throughout our lives. They impact how we think and handle situations as adults.

I recall how humiliating and painful it was as a young person, to wake up in a home with my mother and younger sister and have no heat, electricity, or water in the house. My routine on a cold day was to jump out of bed and head for the floor furnace. One very cold day, I straddled the furnace and it was cold. We later learned that Dad failed to pay the utility bills. He was not around. He was doing his own thing and that didn't involve providing for the needs of his family. I was too young to work and felt helpless to solve the problem. When I did begin working in a grocery store at age 13, it was often my paycheck that provided groceries and utilities. After fifty years of marriage, my family cannot recall one incident of being without utilities.

A friend attended a seminar conducted by a celebrity psychologist. At one point, attendees were asked to raise their hands, if they had been touched inappropriately as a child by an adult. My friend estimated that over 80% of the hands went up. That kind of child abuse is not new, it just went unreported. However, it has a way of shaping our trust. It's not impossible to build a life in which this story can be rewritten. It is difficult. There are many of us, like Jacob after wrestling with the angel, who are walking with a limp.

I was about seven years old and not a swimmer. On a trip to the creek with my sister and the man who would be her husband for 51 years, I stepped into water over my head. I don't recall screaming. I do recall my future brother-in-law bounding into the water and retrieving me.

In middle school, two of my friends lost their lives by drowning. I cannot imagine what might have gone through their minds during their last moments. It puts fear in me, even as an adult. At 17, in Naval basic training, I was required to swim 50 yards. As I crossed the finish line, most of the fear disappeared. Yet the memory of that horrible day at the creek lingers and I do walk with a limp.

Recently, my wife, daughter and I drove by an old house in Fort Worth. Brenda related a horrible memory several times over the years. As we drove by, she recognized the house that she remembered her family visiting with another family. The house was located across from the county hospital emergency room.

When the families finished their visit, everyone got in the car. The father of the other family leaned into the car to talk with Brenda's father. Brenda slammed her door, not realizing the man's hand was where the door closed. She still recalls cutting off the man's fingers. That experience worked its way into her feelings about herself and has taken some work on her part.

The same thing happened to her (minus severing her fingers) years later, when the daughter of some friends caught Brenda's fingers as the car door shut. I stayed with her for hours. The dad in the car had been an Army medic and utilized his knowledge to help her through the initial pain. To this day, she watches closer than anyone else, when a car door is closing. She is not one to take anything for granted.

Another time, Brenda was with other family members in her grandfather's car. He stopped the car for some reason and stepped out. The car began rolling and Brenda reached over to step on the brake. It was not the brake she stepped on, but the accelerator and the car lurched forward. She was scolded dearly by the adults for that. That experience has remained with her.

It was that Sunday morning, when Dad ripped the left front fender off the 1946 Pontiac with his bare hands. He was angry that Mother was taking my sister and me to church. He hated church. I have vivid memories of him threatening to come into the building during church, walking down front, pulling the preacher from the pulpit and beating him up. That was one of his constant threats. When I decided to enter the ministry, Dad was not proud of my choice.

That Sunday still lingers in my memory. Mother drove us to church, with the fender missing from the Pontiac. It took courage. No one asked what happened to the car. What a relief. Mother wouldn't lie, and the truth would be difficult for anyone to handle—but no one asked.

Our neighbors across from us were friends of the family. The daughter is six months older than me and was like a sister as we grew up. The family of four was loading their 1950 Chevrolet for the trip home after church. I jumped in the back seat with the kids, not wanting to go home to an unpredictable afternoon, especially in a car with a missing fender. Mother came to the car and asked me to go with her. I just sat there in defiance. I recall the stern voice of the man driving the car, as he turned around and demanded; "Get out of the car."

That helped shape me. That man was one of my mentors. Mother was going home to face a man who exploded in rage that affected those closest to him. I'm glad I didn't send her and my sister home to deal with it alone. Today, I cannot think of anything I dislike badly enough to leave a negative picture in the minds of my children. It's not about me. I can think of things I have struggled with my entire life and things that have threatened my efforts of being everything I want to be. It is in these things that I depend on God's spirit for strength and His grace in the midst of my imperfections. Christ paid the price for my shortcomings.

Releasing the Past

Some things are precious and worth holding on to. Isn't it amazing to listen to an elderly person detail something that happened on their youngest child's first day of school? What makes it amazing, is the difficulty they have in recalling something discussed yesterday.

Israel continued to complain to Moses. It didn't take them long (even fresh from a victory) to bring up the past, and the past was not so good. These were not very forward-looking people. They complained to Moses, "Why have you brought us out of Egypt to die in the wilderness? There is no bread! There is no water! And we detest this miserable food!" (Numbers 21:5) A life of slavery was better?

It never has been my desire to glorify my past. That is why no hat ever will be on my head that announces my military past. It is an honor to be a veteran. It is not my greatest achievement. A VA doctor oversees my medical care. I receive a free meal on Veterans Day at some restaurants and a small disability payment each month. However, forward is a great direction and I refuse to be captured by the past.

It was radio commentator Paul Harvey, who often stated, "Tomorrow is my favorite day."

The following poem is a reflection on this idea:

Tomorrow is my favorite day,

  I would not look the other way.

As time goes forward in my mind,
> I do not crave a gaze behind.

My greatest hour is yet to be,
> Marking time ahead of me.

Calling me to travel on,
> And set my compass toward the sun.

There's nothing in the past for me,
> But that which served to set me free.

To walk the upward pilgrim way,
> Longing for the better day.

The past I'd rather leave behind,
> The present challenge who can find?

Tomorrow is my favorite day,
> I would not look the other way.

Chapter 22

Vanity Sells

"Don't think you are better than you really are. Be honest in your evaluation of yourselves, measuring yourselves by the faith God has given us."
—Romans 12:3

Greek literature was an enlightening study, especially Narcissus. This was the fellow who was ridiculously handsome. He discovered his good looks, when he saw his reflection in the water. He became enthralled with himself and stared at the image, until he died. It carries over to the fairy tale line "mirror, mirror, on the wall, who's the fairest of them all?"

Research reveals over a hundred identities assumed by the comic strip character Snoopy. From the world-famous surgeon, hockey coach, advice columnist, novel writer (who never seems to get past the opening remarks), a bald eagle, the Statue of Liberty, skating pro, WWI flying ace to Joe Cool, there always seems to be a character he would rather be than himself.

Paul wrote "Don't think you are better than you really are. Be honest in your evaluation of yourselves, measuring yourselves by the faith God has given us." (Romans 12:3)

Most of us live lives, where humility comes and goes. A good friend made his living selling cars and he was very good at it (and honest). He described how he appealed to the vanity of a potential buyer. They would come to him with their heart set on a specific car. My friend would take them for a test drive. His normal route was the business district of the city. It was filled with high rise buildings covered with glass. As they drove by those gleaming buildings, my salesman friend would point to their reflected image in the glass and comment "look over there at how cool you look." That alone closed most sales.

A pair of my jeans had a hole in the leg, when I bought them new. They were priced right and fit well. It was a design in high demand. The manufacturer had convinced buyers that the tattered look is fashionable. That is not what drew me to them. My wrinkled skin is not something I am anxious to show. From clothing to makeup to vehicles, marketers have done an amazing job of appealing to a person's vanity. However, Paul cautioned that vanity is not the measure of our lives.

It might be pants falling off, while holding them with our hand. Perhaps it could be a mullet hairstyle, nose pierced with a ring, earlobe pierced into a large circle, a tattoo on the upper arm shaped like barbed wire or oversized tires on a car. Maybe I am missing something. I don't like unnecessary pain. That is what kept me from coming home from the Navy with a tattoo. I was in a minority, especially as we sailed the Far East on an aircraft carrier. The guys took pride in saying "I got mine in Hong Kong, Sasebo or Okinawa." Some were intriguing, but the stories of pain were not. I wonder who set the standard. I have old family photos from my mothers collection that show the boys in knickers and the girls with Charleston skirts. Who was the first person to come up with the idea and convince everyone else that was a cool thing to do or wear? I'll never know. However, along the way, someone made a good income producing and selling those items.

It's estimated that less than 30% of all off-road trucks are ever driven off-road. Why is it that we spend so much of our time posing, rather than projecting the image of who God created us to be?

A new word that has been added to the English language is the word "selfie." As I was walking on the track at the gym, a college-age girl was walking (slower than me), holding her phone in front of her face and snapping selfies. This usually is done with the "duck face" and two fingers in the "victory" position, next to pursed lips. The neat thing about selfies is that we can take them repeatedly, until we are satisfied that the image is worthy of being posted on social media.

Most amusing to me are the body builders at the gym. I have never understood the value of the large mirrors on the wall. It is amusing to watch the men (I have rarely seen a woman doing this) admiring themselves, as they lift weights. They will sit on the bench, staring at the mirror. I can only imagine what they are admiring.

It becomes a distraction. Paul wrote "Don't copy the behavior and customs of this world, but let God transform you into a new person by changing the way you think. Then you will learn to know God's will for you, which is good and pleasing and perfect." (Romans 12:2) He goes on to say, "Do not think of yourself more highly than you ought, but rather think of yourself with sober judgment."

Why doesn't that deserve more effort on our part, than self-admiration or copying the latest fad?

Posing

John Eldredge refers to it as posing. I keep a photo of our only great-granddaughter Eden on my cell phone. This picture was taken in our kitchen, while she was being held by her dad. She had just turned one and was not in a good mood. When I got my camera pointed at her, she launched into a great big smile. That certainly did not represent her attitude at the moment, but it was a photo worth keeping.

Once I had a photo taken for a company award. We selected a local photographer with many recommendations. After the light was adjusted, he asked me to close my eyes and slowly open them, when he gave the word. It was in the middle of opening my eyes, that he snapped the photo. That process enhanced my appearance in a unique way. I follow this method when I know I am being photographed. I want to look my best.

Maybe appearances are why we reply "fine," when someone asks us how we are doing. We want to appear to others that we are fine. Jeremiah cried out to God "I am ridiculed all day long; everyone mocks me" (Jeremiah 20:7) We hate being mocked so much, that we pose. We want others to see us as we want to be seen—not as we really are.

A study was done regarding the most psychologically well-adjusted people in the world. It was found that symphony orchestra conductors came out on top. Can you envision waiving your arms toward the people surrounding you and having them respond exactly as you want? Having everything go my way, certainly has not brought out the best in me. Struggling against challenges and enduring hardship has.

It took Joseph twenty-two years preparing for the outcome that God had in mind. He ended up as Number Two in Egypt under Pharaoh, but most of those years were spent with his life on the line. How can I expect anything more?

Jesus warned about projecting a false image. In Matthew 6:2, He says "So when you give to the needy, do not announce it with trumpets, as the hypocrites do in the synagogues, and on the streets, to be honored by others." He also condemned false displays of righteousness when he said "Everything they do is done for people to see. They make phylacteries wide and the tassels on their garments long." (Matthew 23:5)

Why are we not content with who we are? "Whoever wants to be my disciple must deny themselves and take up their cross daily and follow me" (Luke 9:23) There is nothing wrong with "who we are." Yet we spend far too much of our time attempting to be someone we are not, because we envision their lives as better than our own.

The false image and the real person are always at odds. More effort is required to project a perceived image, than to develop what already is in the person's nature.

Look at a group picture that includes you. Your eyes usually will go directly to the spot where you are standing. If we are asked about the welfare of our children, we certainly will not present them as disappointments. We will hold them up as highly successful, so others will consider us to be capable parents.

As I prepare to conduct a funeral, I am continually stunned that the family spokesperson (often with the help of other family members) produces a list of traits that celebrates the uniqueness of that person and how they stood out to them. In every case, I wonder how often they communicated that uniqueness and value to the person, who can no longer hear it.

When I draw my last breath, I will not be judged for how well I have copied the life and achievements of someone else. I will be giving an account of how I brought glory to the God who created me with what He gave me. No one else can be me.

Chapter 23

Learning the Hard Way

"Jesus told him, 'Stand up, pick up your mat, and walk.' Instantly, the man was healed! He rolled up his sleeping mat and began walking!" —John 5:8-9

It's the way I've learned the most. I entered college looking for my questions to be answered. A wise professor responded to intense questions by a student once, by saying, "We don't teach you to give you all the answers. Our job is to teach you where to go search for the answers you are looking for." My immediate response to that in my mind was "what a cop out." If someone has the answer to something, why doesn't he just spout it out?

While I never took a class from the dean, we became friends and preached for neighboring churches. The dean would joke, "Tom and I are co-bishops in Tate County, Mississippi."

On a visit to his office one day, I asked him for a quick answer. "What is the unpardonable sin?" It is mentioned in Matthew 12:32: "Anyone who speaks a word against the Son of Man will be forgiven, but anyone who speaks against the Holy Spirit will not be forgiven, either in this age or in the age to come." Everything learned from scripture had given assurance that there is no sin that is too big for God to forgive. The dean replied, "That is a good question. I'd like you to write a research paper on that question and tell me what you learn."

I did. I answered my own question. Not long after that, I went to him and asked another question. You would think I would know better by now.

That's pretty much been the story of my life—LEARNING THE HARD

WAY. It was a biblical professor in my undergraduate study who thrived on short (to the point) research reporting. He assigned a research paper once a week. His instructions were to limit the paper to three typewritten pages—not two and a half or three and a fourth, but exactly three. It became a lesson in extreme discipline to say what needs to be said and not waste words.

Life is a lot like that as well, isn't it? Paul thought so. Brenda's favorite verse is: "I know what it is to be in need, and I know what is to have plenty. I have learned the secret of being content in any and every situation, whether well fed or hungry, whether living in plenty or in want." Paul had it figured out and it came to him the hard way.

It is the next statement that captured my wife: "I can do all this through him who gives me strength." How did he receive the strength? Through some divine revelation? Through a dream? Heavens no. I stood over the spot in Rome which is said to be this apostle's final resting place. My admiration for him is what led me to ask Brenda if we could name our son after him. He learned a great deal in life by experiencing it. So, do we. It is an effective way to learn what life can bring and the capability and desire of a loving God who can carry us through anything.

Weeping with Those Who Weep

When someone asks if life is supposed to be fair, my answer is, "If so, then fairness has eluded me." When I am overwhelmed, I recall Job. He is one of the heroes at the top of my list. I stand on Proverbs 2:20, "…walk in the steps of good men." Job is one of my mentors. For the most part, I desperately want to respond to hardship, as Job did.

I often wonder how effective I am at reaching out to someone who is hurting. I wondered that recently, when the officer and I went to the county hospital. We were sent to guard a female (probably around 50). Her lifestyle was obvious by her rough appearance. She was there because she had threatened to jump off a building to end her life. In between nurse visits, I talked with her as much as possible.

"My name is Tom and I am here with this officer—what's your name?" No response. I gently looked at her arm bracelet for her name. I made direct eye contact, as she lay secured to the gurney by a handcuff.

"Jill (not her real name). I see your name is Princess Jill. You are more important than we expected. My boss sent me with a message for you. You are extremely valuable and that is why you have been given the title princess." She needed additional attention and eventually was taken to another part of the hospital. That is when I walked away and asked God to take over.

At this time in our lives, the most effective comfort for us is a word from God. That word might come through a person or their presence alone. It is less effective, when it consists of advice on how to get through it all—especially if that person has not experienced anything similar.

In New Testament times, mourning often was done in an organized way. Part of the process was to hire professional mourners. These people could express grief over the death of another person, without even knowing who they were. Although it added to the atmosphere of grief, it is difficult to imagine that it was very effective. Those who help the most, always are those who know the deceased in a personal way and give accounts of how they had interacted, how important they were to them and how they would remember them.

We look for the right words to reach out to those who are hurting. Silence is often the best choice. Jackie was a wife and mother. Her husband and two children were hospitalized at the same time—her husband with a life-threatening heart condition. She didn't need an attempt by anyone to make a sympathetic phone call. She was not certain what she needed from anyone else.

Value of Time

Jim Croce was 29 when his music took off. Bad, Bad Leroy Brown was getting recognition and sending Jim on a demanding concert schedule. He was missing his wife. His hit song Time in a Bottle had become a great sing along piece, that carried a significant message.

If I could save time in a bottle, the first thing that I'd like to do.

Is to save every day till eternity passes away, just to spend them with you.

If I could make days last forever, if words could make wishes come true.

I'd save every day like a treasure and again, I would spend them with you.

> *But there never seems to be enough time, to do the things you want to do.*

> *Once I've looked around enough to know when you're the one I want to go through time with.*

If I had a box just for wishing and dreams that had never come true.

> *The box would be empty except for the memory of how they were answered by you.*

I would like for you to read those words once more. Beginning with my wife, each child, grandchild, great-grandchild, sister, niece, nephew, friend and those who have crossed paths with me. You are what my life has been about, and I am committed to not messing it up.

I write this in the aftermath of the passing of my friend Kenny. At his request, I will give the message at his funeral service. Time has been our ally for over seventy years. It has served its purpose and now it's time to move on. All that's left are memories and the influence that had a part in shaping me.

When Solomon became king, God offered to grant him any request he made. He simply asked for wisdom and knowledge to serve effectively as king. All I expected from Kenny was friendship. God gave much more. Similar to David and Jonathan (1Samuel 18:1), Kenny and I became one in spirit. I have loved him as myself. I experienced the same in return. When he told me that he would not be receiving additional treatment for his cancer, I apologized to him for spending all those years without having a spiritual conversation. That changed. We both spoke the words "I love you" many times and shared our confidence in God's forgiveness. We anticipate the continuation of this friendship in a new place, where brokenness will not distract.

I was on scene with two officers. A young boy turned at a busy intersection and struck an adult bicycle rider. He stopped, and we came upon the accident, before an emergency call could be made. The bike rider needed no medical attention. Even with a superior officer, blame could not be placed. I struck up a conversation with the boy and his mother. Both were distraught. I looked at the boy and assured him that he was to be commended for stopping and assuming responsibility for his part in the accident. No one could be cited for negligence. In the presence of the young man, Mom and I agreed that her son would always recall this experience. It would be something that would help to shape his future as a driver and a person. As we were leaving, the boy reached out to shake my hand and his mom thanked me for "the kind words."

I merely sought to speak something comforting at a stressful time. I received assurance of much more. That is how life has played out so far with the God of Abraham, Isaac, Jacob, and Tom. I expect it to continue to do so.

Chapter 24

I Don't Have Time for This

"For there is a right time and way for everything, even if a man's trouble is heavy upon him." —Ecclesiastes 8:6

He is one of the godliest men I know. He is generous, loving, merciful and comes from a godly family. My friend is someone who can be trusted to do what he says. At breakfast, we opened our hearts about the heaviest burdens we are carrying. I know of no safer place to talk about these things. He trusts me as well. I called him to share the news of my wife's cancer diagnosis.

He shared with me a similar diagnosis—involving him. His doctors have a plan, but it will seriously interrupt his own plans. Not long ago, he sold his unique business to dedicate his life to ministry. This will change things. He told me outright, "I don't have time for this." The wheels have been turning in my mind since then.

Since when does a challenge like this come at a convenient time? I was moved by a police memorial published in the paper. An officer lost his life at the hands of a person full of hate, leaving children without a father. When he left that morning, he made it a point to kiss his children. Families of police officers are aware of the dangers that they face every day. Nevertheless, they live with the assumption that Daddy will be coming home at the end of his day. It is a shock of unimaginable proportions to receive word that he won't be coming home. These children will go through school, graduate, begin a family and have children who only will hear stories of their grandfather.

It is a tragedy that this father was taken from his children. He WAS involved in the lives of his children and they are going to miss out on a lot. However, I am persuaded that God will compensate and bless them with opportunities they otherwise would not have had.

A good friend told me of his father joining the military at the beginning of the Korean conflict. (It is amazing that a man in his seventies would confide an account such as this to a friend years later). My friend's dad never returned. Both he and his brother grew up without a dad and both thrived in the medical field. The absence of a parent didn't cause life to stop for them.

My dad lived to be 76, but for the most part, I grew up without him. He was gone a lot with his own agenda. When he was home, he was not attentive to his children. I dreaded the nights when he would drink too much. He might as well have not been there. I recall numerous times I preferred him not to be. I was trying to grow up and didn't have time for this. He left for California, when I was fourteen. I don't recall being sad, I just knew I would no longer be coming home to a father who was out of control because of alcohol.

I read a very sad obituary. "Leslie passed away on January 30, 2017, which was 29 years longer than expected and much longer than he deserved.... He leaves behind two relieved children...along with six grandchildren and countless other victims including an ex-wife...At a young age, Leslie quickly became a model example of bad parenting...and a complete commitment to drinking, drugs, womanizing and being generally offensive...Leslie's hobbies included being abusive to his family, expediting trips to heaven for the beloved family pets and fishing...Leslie's life served no other obvious purpose. He did not contribute to society or serve his community and he possessed no redeeming qualities, besides quick-witted sarcasm which was amusing during his sober days...With Leslie's passing, he will be missed only for what he never did; being a loving husband, father and good friend...No services will be held, there will be no prayers for eternal peace and no apologies to the family he tortured...Leslie's passing proves that evil does in fact die and hopefully marks a time of healing and safety for all."

Imagine the effort it took for Leslie to be that bad. It reminds me of Mark Antony's speech at the death of Julius Caesar which I memorized in high school: "The evil that man does lives after him: the good is oft interred in his bones." Pain and heartache indeed live on in the lives of victims. Leslie (like all of us) was given an entire lifetime to make good choices and leave a positive legacy for those who wanted him to love them. How sad that he used so much energy and so many resources to choose otherwise.

Another family published their mother's obituary; "In 1962 she became pregnant by her husband's brother. She abandoned her children...who were then raised by her parents...She passed away on May 31 and will now face judgment. She will not be missed by her children, who understand this world is a better place without her." This is a very isolated situation. Death usually is hard.

Very few of the funeral services I perform involve a family who had time to prepare for what they now are facing. Families set up their expected stories involving things as they are. Visit a hospital full of sick people or a children's hospital, where children are being treated for diseases no one anticipated. Life can change on a dime and no one has time for the challenges.

The Baggage We Carry

I was talking with a police friend at another officer's retirement party. I brought up a conversation just an hour before with another person, whose marriage failed in the midst of his wife's serious illness. The officer and I were discussing how that could be avoided. We knew that the divorce rate outside and inside the church are tied at 50%. During their training, police officers are warned that (if they are married) many would be affected by the stress of the job and could be divorced within five years. Many of the officers recall that class session very well. Some have told me that they went home with their wives and committed to beat the odds.

I have read that the presence of a serious illness increases the divorce rate to 80%. Included is the disability of one of the partners, serious illness, or death of a child or perhaps an indiscretion of one of the partners. The man assured me that my wife and I have a much smaller risk of a failed marriage, due to the length of time we have been married. If we have survived this long, likely it will endure for life.

My friend was 50, when he married. I joked, "Maybe it would be best to wait until fifty to marry in order to dispose of baggage." He smiled and said, "Because we waited, we brought a lot of baggage with us."

Couples grow in their relationships with time. Gary Chapman refers to the first two years of marriage, as "the tingles." The tingles are replaced by something deeper that will sustain the relationship. That is the reason for the vows in the beginning. Our vulnerability never escapes God. Validation from the heavenly father comes from humility; "Humble yourselves before the Lord and He will lift you up." (1 Peter 5:6, James 4:10)

Brenda and I visit my sister in the rehab facility she currently calls "home." It inspires me when her roommate's husband comes to dinner with his wife, who has dementia. He pushes her to the dining room, cuts her food and feeds her one bite at a time. It is likely that if the situation were reversed, the wife would be just as attentive. It is inspiring to watch that kind of response to a commitment that was made years ago.

It Keeps Coming

We were asked to pray for a young lady. A rare disease resulted in the amputation of both legs below the knees. A subsequent request was to pray for an additional surgical procedure that would remove both arms. The prayers requested was that the amputation be below the elbows. The prayers worked. The prayers continue, only now the request is that God reveals himself in this experience and His glory will have an everlasting effect on this family. Those of us not affected can go about our daily routine and shudder whenever the thought crosses our mind. Certainly, it is an opportunity to consider Romans 8:28, "We know that all things work together for them that know the Lord."

Let's not stop there. Verse 29 tells me "For God knew his people in advance, and he chose them to become like his Son, so that his Son would be the firstborn." We need look no further for the desired outcome of any suffering experience. God wants us to be like his Son. Being lord of my own life doesn't work—never has—never will. Jesus is the only one worthy of that position and being like Him is the Father's ultimate goal for us in this life.

Matters such as these get no press. Yet the news media becomes obsessed with the misbehavior of a celebrity. A child can be taken from this world prematurely and God is chastised.

It likely is best to keep some issues close to home. It is frightening to think of what social media might do with news of "off the charts" suffering. Those who strike out at God's goodness appear to be confident in their conclusions. I (on the other hand) am forced to reconcile the presence of suffering with the existence of a good, powerful, and loving God. I am not confident enough in my own ability to navigate life alone at the helm.

While Brenda was confined to the cancer floor, I made my daily visits to the coffee shop across the street in the children's hospital. Not once did I make that trip without being surrounded by parents and their children who were there for treatment of diseases that were interfering with their life. Mom and/or Dad are unable to go to work, often traveling from their home in another town, the children reacting violently to the treatments. I cannot escape the presence of suffering. It's all around. My faith is stretched on a daily basis, because I accept the existence of God as He is described in Scripture. It is extremely difficult for me to accept difficult things, since they come with the conclusion "it is what it is." But with God factored in there is hope.

It wasn't only David, who saw the value in suffering. (Psalms 119:71) The writer of Hebrews wrote that Jesus "learned obedience by what He suffered" (Hebrews 5:8) Jesus warned that it would happen. "You will be handed over to the courts and will be flogged with whips in the synagogues. You will stand trial before governors and kings because you are my followers." He gave them His perspective of these experiences: "...this will be your opportunity to tell the rulers and other unbelievers about me." (Matthew 10:16–18)

We are not immune to persecution for following Jesus. 2 Timothy 3:12 makes this promise: "Everyone who wants to live a godly life in Christ will be persecuted." Neither are we protected from the things that characterize the world in which we live. Sickness and death are all around us. Innocent people suffer. Our bodies get old and cause pain and discomfort. Yet we are overcome with inspiration, when we see someone find joy in the midst of pain.

I love to hear stories of how someone refused to allow a challenging experience to defeat them. It confirms that IT CAN BE DONE.

I would never suggest that getting through these off the chart experiences is easy. There are experiences we face that we never could get through alone. I read a quote, "…there are horrors no human heart is equipped to bear." No credit was given to this quote, but I thought it was well said.

Mother had a saying, "Let go and let God." To this day, I am not certain about the practical application of that quote. Mother endured some severe struggles. She was married to an unfaithful man, who abused alcohol and deserted his family. She was left with two young children but never sat back and expected God to bail her out. She worked hard for minimum wage (having only completed ninth grade) and provided effective examples and opportunities for her two kids to associate with people, whose example was worthy to be followed. I learned that 1. I could not count on smooth sailing and that 2. Any insecurity I might have of God's ability and willingness to walk with me is my fault—not His.

Memories are nice, but I love today. I love what I see in my wife, children, grandchildren and great-grandchildren. Many things in the past were painful but we are better for them. We celebrate today. Some memories were sweet and worth holding on to. However, life is not meant to be lived in the past.

Paul wrote "Not that I have already obtained all this, or have already arrived at my goal, but I press on to take hold of that for which Christ Jesus took hold of me. Brothers and sisters, I do not consider myself yet to have taken hold of it. But one thing I do: Forgetting what is behind and straining toward what is ahead, I press on toward the goal to win the prize for which God has called me heavenward in Christ Jesus." (Philippians 3:12–14)

Chapter 25

Blessed Are the Peacemakers

"Blessed are the peacemakers..." —Matthew 5:9

It is beyond my comprehension that the men and women in blue spend their 40-hour work week in that arena exclusively. There are occasions where an officer will locate a missing person, help someone to a safe place after an accident, or give a lost and distraught person a ride home. I love it when an officer attempts to pay for his meal and the cashier tells him someone paid it for him. These are rare but welcomed experiences for these peacekeepers.

I can be with an officer on a crime scene and the vision haunts me for weeks. A week or so after the event, the memory has completely left the officer. Law enforcement work can be very difficult on marriages. Individuals who do that work, have a divine gift indeed.

Much of what I witness when I am along, is someone taking something that is not theirs, causing harm to another person out of momentary rage, or damage to property that is not theirs. These are choices that cannot be reversed. The damage endures for a long time. Proverbs 22:3 declares "A prudent person foresees danger and takes precautions. The simpleton goes blindly on and suffers the consequences."

The Suffering of Consequences

Once the officer I was with was looking for an individual he had dealt with previously. He brought up his photo on the computer screen and explained this man knocked out all of his girlfriend's teeth. She was in the hospital with her injuries. "And she still is his girlfriend?" I questioned. I grew up around domestic abuse and determined not to copy that behavior, regardless of what it took on my part. I married a girl who was the only girl in a family of six kids. She can handle herself. Frankly, I never had the courage to give it a go.

An article in a police publication addressed the maintenance of the "human fleet." A comparison was made to the importance of maintaining the vehicles we drive. There are systems in place that help "maintain and care properly for the fleet of humans, who drive the patrol cars and do this uniquely complex work."

Dr. Kevin Gilmartin noted that officers at all ranks must operate in a physical state known as hypervigilance, in order to be safe and effective in their work. "Hypervigilance is a physiological response to risk in the work environment." There are two extreme responses. One is those who cope with the effects of hypervigilance and become successful in their work and families. The opposite is those who cope through addiction, emotional and family stress - even suicide.

In a 2017 study reported by the *US News and World Report,* it was noted the suicide rate among first responders is more than ten times greater than that of the general population. That is attributed to the effects of what they see in the course of their day. In the middle of these extremes, are those who suffer on their own and experience sleep disorders, cardiopulmonary problems, habitual use of nicotine, alcohol, caffeine, steroids and other harmful substances. The article refers to a study by Dr. John Violanti on the effects of "unmanaged exposure to the unique occupational stress of law enforcement work" and how it (if it remains unmanaged) "puts personnel at significantly increased risk for a host of diseases and disorders."

I take issue with those who say just stop it. God has walked with me through numerous stresses in life. For many, there is the perception that each day of our lives will be equivalent to a trip to Disneyworld. If not, then we just need to "cowboy/cowgirl up" and "get over it." For those of us who struggle to make this happen, our faith is often questioned, or we may even question the presence, compassion or power of God. As I read the book of Job, it is obvious this suffering individual asked God some pointed questions. His friends gave him no comfort at all. Their advice to him, was to examine his life to see what he had done to cause his suffering. After all, don't we get what we deserve? "Don't be misled—you cannot mock the justice of God. You will always harvest what you plant." (Galatians 6:7)

Without going into a major discourse on this subject, I simply will mention that Jesus did nothing to deserve what He received. Neither did John the Baptizer who lost his head, or Stephen who was stoned to death, or the Apostle Paul who was beaten and imprisoned for declaring the message of salvation from God.

I am grateful that churches have counselors on staff. My family has made use of these helpful individuals. We are aware of what the scriptures say, and the numerous promises recorded. Even so, I have never found that our lives have avoided pitfalls and we have experienced hurt and disappointment over the way life has gone.

Car burglaries are up significantly in our city. With an officer taking a report on a home break-in, I am crushed that these people must live in the house or drive the car that has been violated by someone they do not know. At nine years of age, my friend and I stole an inexpensive toy from a toy store. The owner knew our parents and called them. After being confronted by my mother, we were taken to the store to apologize to the owner. My friend's dad was a business owner and a prince of a man (one of the good men in my life of Proverbs 2:20). My companion in wrong-doing told me it was the first time he had ever seen his dad cry. I have a serious aversion to holding something in my hand, that is not rightfully mine. I count the change that comes out of the cash register. Occasionally, it gives me a little too much and I hand it to the attendant. I cannot force myself to keep something that belongs to someone else. I have a difficult time understanding how anyone can sleep, knowing they have violated another person by taking what that other person worked for.

They wouldn't like it, if someone did it to them. Surely, the golden rule applies.

My heart aches for the person who is about to get news of a deceased family member. It was my wife who told me my brother had died in an auto accident. Years later, she delivered the news of the death of another significant mentor. This man was priceless during one of the most difficult transitions of my life and our marriage. It has been more than twenty years. Sometimes I drive to the country cemetery, where he is buried. I sit under the tree next to his grave; talk to him and thank God for sending this person my way at a crucial time. I hear accounts of how a loved one appears in a dream, long after they are gone. Such a separation leaves severe emptiness and we are never ready.

I was on the list of ministers on call to fill in at a hospital, while the chaplain was going through cancer treatment. I received a call one day asking my help in a situation I had feared for a long time. A young man was driving on a trip with his mother. He had been sleeping in the back seat of the car, while his mother drove. She became very tired, woke him and asked him if he was rested enough take over. He assured her that he was. Just a few minutes after they got back on the road, he fell asleep, wrecked the car and his mother was pronounced dead at the scene. I was briefed on the situation, as I walked into the emergency room with the highway patrolman who had worked the accident. We stood beside the young man's bed. The trooper did a masterful job explaining to the young man that his mother did not survive. I keep a picture in my mind of his reaction. He blamed his own carelessness for his mother's death. I was relieved that the job of informing him fell to the trooper and not the minister. That still is the protocol in the police work I do today. These officers are trained to do this. I hope I never am called upon for that task. If so, I don't want to mess it up.

An Officer's Perspective

One of my favorite officers raised a familiar objection. It is one that I have wrestled with myself. "I don't claim to be religious and there are some issues that make no sense to me. I look at all of those who are suffering (including children). I have a friend who has been fighting cancer. We deal with a lot of head-on car crashes that are alcohol-related and in most of those, the intoxicated driver survives, while the other driver does not."

I knew where he was going, because I often go there myself. I completed the thought: "If there is a God who created the universe and he loves us and has the power to prevent this kind of evil, why doesn't he?"

"Exactly!"

I explained that I returned from the military with severe doubts about the existence of God. During college, I saw an opportunity to study (at the graduate level) the subject of Christian Apologetics. I needed to make sense of all the hurt and pain in a world created by a God who has the power to stop it. Why doesn't he? I saw the possibility of some understanding—but never found it. Humility resulted, as well as spiritual growth and wisdom. I still cannot give a convincing explanation of why God doesn't put an end to the horrible things that go on in this world—at least one that would convince others. *Let them happen to the evil people and leave the good people alone.* That makes more sense to me.

For a person who spends his work days around people who choose evil, I understand the struggle. I face it myself. They see people who choose behaviors that bring hurt to themselves and others, that cannot be reversed. To raise enough money to purchase illegal drugs, someone points a gun at an innocent person, the gun discharges and the person is killed or wounded. Lives are changed forever. The perpetrator must live with that bad decision for the rest of his life.

I know officers who see God's way, as the only reasonable choice. They are not willing to blame God for the bad behavior of humans. We all have free will. Some have shared with me extremely painful experiences they only survived by their faith in God. I know it is possible.

It doesn't seem fair, does it? A mother taken from her young children. A child subjected to a horrible illness. A soldier living with a disability caused years ago in a war.

Negative news: a man allegedly holds a teen captive for months and impregnates her; the founder of a non-profit for at-risk boys arrested for soliciting explicit photos from a child; a church founder given 40 years in prison for sexual relations with two teenage girls; a suspected serial rapist arrested at a bus station; a woman forces her way into the apartment of an elderly man, beats and robs him a few days later.

In every case, my heart aches for the families of those victims. It is no secret that if we live long enough, we will be separated from someone we love. However, never in our wildest imagination, do we dream it would be at the hands of someone who has allowed their mind to be distorted by illegal drugs or simply has grown into an adult with little conscience.

No Family Is Spared

My mother told me of an uncle, who once attended an auction where he sold several items. On the way home, he was robbed and murdered by someone who stole the money he earned. This was before I was born and before automobiles were prevalent. He was on horseback. However, the image of this tragic event implanted empathy in my young mind for those in my family I had learned to love. This man was their close relative.

In my early twenties, I received word that one of my mother's two brothers in Tennessee had been hit by a car and died. It was a hit and run situation. A police officer saw it, left his car at the scene and chased the offender on foot. The driver was arrested in his garage at home. My brother called to tell me of this. This uncle was not one of our favorite people, but he was part of the family.

We look with disdain on the one who caused such damage in the life of another. What about the parents of that individual? What about the parents of the Boston Strangler, John Wilkes Booth, Lee Harvey Oswald and the host of lesser-known persons who have hurt others? How do these parents handle the unexpected actions of this person they once rejoiced over at birth, nurtured and spent time dreaming of their future?

I know it is difficult—especially for a mother. She is the one who endured the pain of childbirth. She is the one who changed them, bathed them, fed them, cared for them when they were sick, and watched them go to school on their first day. A clear memory remains of my sister's youngest child going off to kindergarten on the opening day of school. I was riding along. My sister burst into tears and cried, as she escorted her son up the walk. That boy is sixty now and overseeing his mother's care in assisted living. We sit with her as she tells stories about his childhood, as though it were yesterday. The details are uncanny.

Peacemaking in All Forms

The incarcerated juveniles submit a new list of prayer requests to their chaplain:

- I hope and pray that my mama becomes un-incarcerated and can get me back home.

- Pray that my uncle gets out of prison and that I can go home before Thanksgiving.

- Pray that I can go home with my family to help my mom to take stress off of her.

- Pray that my granny gets better, and for God to watch over my family. And be with me and my brother on our court dates.

- Pray that I will not get a determinate sentence to TJJD, (Juvenile Justice Detention). Also, bless my family and the ones I dislike.

The only way the past will serve these young offenders, is to bring about a better future. It is expected that they will walk into their future with a limp. Jacob carried with him effects of the wound he received from his encounter with God's angel. "And he was limping because of his hip." (Genesis 32:31) But that is what Jesus does —offers us freedom from the effects of our past. Who can deny that Jacob (Israel) made good use of his life despite his limp?

It was the officer I was with, who said it. A man named Robert had harmed himself more than once. There were self-inflicted injuries on his head, face and arm. The man blamed himself for several things that had gone wrong in his life. The officer told Robert, "There is not anything that can't be forgiven." Robert needed to hear that.

"Robert, I'm a minister and I spend a lot of time with these officers. My boss has sent me to you with a message. Do you know who my boss is?" A finger rises from his hands that are bound with handcuffs. The finger points upward. "You are right, Robert. My boss has sent me to tell you how valuable you are. You are far more valuable than you think—and every time you hurt yourself, he hurts too."

Robert had made some statements to the officers, indicating he had a spiritual perspective (I was baptized twice, etc.). I took a chance and jumped in. We discussed Satan's tactics and how Satan was the real enemy, not Robert. We prayed right there, as Robert sat in the back seat of a police car tightly holding my hand with both of his. We commanded Satan to leave Robert alone in the name of Jesus Christ. Heaven will reveal the outcome of this encounter.

A girl in her middle teens, reported an assault on the school bus. When we arrived, another officer and two ambulance attendants were in the living room. The mother was weak from chemotherapy treatments. The daughter was demanding to be taken for medical attention, even after the EMT (after careful examination) assured her that her nose was not broken. A trip to the hospital would place her mother at risk. In her weakened state, she could easily become sick being around other sick people. The girl could not go without her mother. This girl was wearing an ankle monitor; she had been on probation since the age of twelve. The ambulance attendants told her that they were receiving other calls and needed to go. I cannot recall when I last listened to a teenager scream at their mother, as loudly as this one did.

As we drove away, the mother was backing out the family car to take her daughter to an emergency room. Rebellious teenager wins again. These situations leave families scarred, as well as communities.

Christmas season brings an increase in domestic issues, suicide attempts and deaths—many at their own hand. All the joy and celebration around the Christmas season seems evasive. Many become disenchanted and feel singled out for a life of loneliness and despair.

In a recent obituary, a brilliant man's family related his own admission regarding his addiction. It was due to a life less than what he had imagined when younger. By his own admission, he allowed his light to go out, by failing to live the life of which he was capable.

What are we expecting out of life anyway? If we compare ourselves to others, we always will come up short. Press is given to those in this world who need not DO anything. They merely are expected to BE. Many are descendants of royalty, married to royalty or offspring of royalty, extreme wealth or celebrity. Nothing has earned them the position. Most of us are in the position of earning our way and most of us will never be in the right place at the right time. That, however, does not take away our value.

On a call with an officer, we encountered a situation that would break the heart of any parent. Father and son were sitting on the couch. The son was deceased. I followed the father out the door and did my best to speak with him. The effort was limited, since the words did not come from an emotional level which matched that of the father. It rarely does.

A bystander recorded the entire incident of a couple arguing outside a building. The couple had been together for a year and she was pregnant. He began strangling her. When we arrived with another police car to assist, the officers placed handcuffs on him and had the female sit on the curb. I listened to her story. As always, it was different from his.

Families continue to hurt. Five families were intact, with their lives moving along normally. Then a couple of days later, a pilot goes down in the aircraft he was flying. Later, a high-profile tragic incident took the lives of five policemen in a major city. When they left home for work that day, there was no reason to expect the day to be different from any other. It became the day of separation from their loved ones. Two of them lived a short distance from my family. How many times did they stop their car to let me go by, because I had the right of way? How many times did we pass each other in the store or post office? They are now gone from here. We are left to contemplate the pain and emptiness in their families. Having been separated from several members of my family through the years, I can identify with those hurting families better than in the beginning when I had experienced nothing of the sort. We have no right to be pharisaical about it and say, "Thank God it did not happen in my family." It is my obligation to use the days I have been given, to reflect the image of Jesus in an effective way. This is my final gift.

There is an offender in the loss of life of those police officers. The young man had grown bitter, over the behavior of others. Such a response is wrong. It is not my job to retaliate against the citizens of Germany for victims of the Holocaust. I was born on the very day the Japanese bombed Pearl Harbor. Eighteen years later, the Navy sent me to live in Japan for two years. I never felt one twinge of an obligation to take revenge on these people. "Do not take revenge, my dear friends, but leave room for God's wrath, for it is written, 'it is mine to avenge; I will repay,' says the Lord." (Romans 12:19)

The news reported that this bitter young man was living with his mother and not much was published about her. Is it okay for our thoughts to wander toward her? This is certainly a shock to the purpose she had for this child. The father of this young man was quoted as saying "I love my son, but I am not proud of what he did." How many of us can say that about our own children? How many times does God say that about us? There is a third party here. It is Satan. It is his job to discredit God. It is our job to resist Satan (James 4:7)

Words of comfort spoken today were not learned in college, graduate school or numerous books read. The "Crisis Intervention" class comes up short in providing the skills needed to comfort another person, who is in the first moments of a severe crisis. It is part of living in this world and it won't quit until our lives do. That does not make it hurt any less.

I spend a lot of time with police officers. We encounter citizens facing severe pain. I tell these officers that they are my post-graduate professors. I didn't learn any of this in college nor did I learn how to react or what to say (or when to remain silent) from a text book.

My journey is continuous. I am the one responsible for progress. I only can make an effort to bridge the gap between the hurting person and the only one who has the ability to bring healing. Life has no "search" mechanism that yields instant answers. Neither is there a "delete" button that will undo mistakes or their consequences. God is the master teacher. He walks through the fire with us when we ask and sometimes when we don't ask.

This reminds me of the time our family was visiting Galveston, Texas. Our youngest child (Amber) ran ahead of us, as we crossed a busy street. She was focused on the beach on the other side. I reached out and grabbed her arm, just in time to keep her from being struck by a car she did not see. God has done that to me time and time again.

I am moved by a new story about a husband, father, and grandfather that lost his life, when hit by a car. As usual, the timing was horrible. He was a good man living by good principles. The wife made it a point to hold harmless and forgive the person driving the car that struck her husband. This is another good person who lifts my heart. We live in a broken world and are subject to hurt. However, as long as grace and forgiveness are present, we can endure.

Satan will have success for a time, but we know the final outcome: "Every knee will bow, and every tongue will confess that Jesus is Lord." We can pick our team now.

Chapter 26

Where Do We Go from Here?

"We must work the works of him who sent me while it is day; night is coming, when no one can work." —John 9:4

I love 1 Kings 19. Elijah was chosen to deal with Ahab and his wicked wife Jezebel. However, Elijah was a whiner. Why would anyone with an assignment directly from God complain? Ahab was a wicked king married to a very wicked woman. That's quite a combination for a position of leadership, isn't it? Just read the account in 1 Kings 21 of Ahab taking the vineyard of a good man, Nabal, just because he wanted to. That makes my blood boil.

Nothing Elijah told Ahab was received with favor. Ahab and Jezebel couldn't wait to get their hands on this man of God and silence him forever. Everywhere Elijah turned, he was met with resistance. God found him sulking. Jezebel had threatened his life and "Elijah was afraid and ran for his life. When he came to Beersheba in Juda, he left his servant there, while he himself went a day's journey into the wilderness. He came to a broom bush, sat down under it and prayed that he might die. 'I have had enough Lord,' he said. Take my life; I am no better than my ancestors." Even after three powerful demonstrations of God's presence, Elijah whined, "I have been very zealous for the Lord God Almighty. The Israelites have rejected your covenant, torn down your altars, and put your prophets to death with the sword, I am the only one left, and now they are trying to kill me too." (Verses 10–14)

The story ends in victory; God won, and Elijah made history. You would think that if God were going to send Elijah on such a mission, He would "Make straight paths for him." (Isaiah 40:3, Mark 1:3) This was said on behalf of John the Baptizer, as he was sent on a mission to prepare for the ministry of Jesus. However, John was put in prison for his efforts and eventually beheaded. How fair is that? I do not find any promise in all of scripture that guarantees smooth sailing for those carrying out the Lord's mission. There is one promise we can count on. "Everyone who wants to live a godly life in Christ Jesus, will be persecuted. (2 Timothy 3:12)

Watching Others

Watching others has been a big help to me. It also has been a hindrance, at times eliciting the temptation to invent shortcomings. No one handles things well because they are being watched. In fact, I suspect when most of us go through trials, we question how well we handled it. We can't really know, until it is over and that may not even be in this life.

One of my life mentors came into my family, when I was very young. He became our family doctor. His family was active in the same church and his oldest son and I were the same age. The son and I became friends, attended school together, were Boy Scouts and sometimes I spent the night at his house. His dad became one of our scout leaders and did physicals for all of us, who went away to camp. I recall walking a trail with the doctor at camp. He abruptly reached down and grabbed me by the arm, to prevent me from taking another step. When I looked, I noticed a copperhead snake in my path.

About the time I was a teenager; Mother came to me and described a terrible tragedy in the family of this doctor. The mother and her two sons were involved in a car crash that took the life of the mother. It seemed unfathomable for two young boys to have their mother taken at such a young age—especially before their eyes. My friend was affected terribly.

The good doctor carried on. Soon after this tragedy, he partnered with two other physicians to form a medical school in the city where he practiced. The school began in a building that had been a bowling alley.

This doctor met and married a fine woman and continued to serve as a leader in the church. Several years later, his second wife preceded him in death. He continued to work on developing the medical school, while maintaining his practice. Eventually, he met and married a third fine woman. This good doctor was preceded in death by his third wife.

I attended a reception in his honor. Although by then in a wheel chair, he still had his usual firm grip and told me how happy he was to see me.

I attended his memorial service and saw only a few people I knew. His name adorns the building at the Medical School campus (a far cry from the original bowling alley). It was years into adulthood, that I encountered the passage in Proverbs 2:20 "Walk in the steps of good men." This good doctor was one of these. I can see a bit of him in every step I take today.

Aristotle is given credit for teaching Alexander the Great. History bears witness to this leader's accomplishments at a very young age. He found himself on his deathbed at the age of 33.

Summoning his generals, he made three requests:

1. The best doctors should carry his coffin.

2. The wealth he had accumulated, should be scattered along the procession to the cemetery.

3. His hands should be left loose, hanging outside the coffin for all to see.

One general had the courage to request an explanation. Alexander explained:

1. I want the best doctors to carry my coffin to demonstrate that, in the face of death, even the best doctors in the world have no power to heal.

2. I want the road to be covered with my treasure, so that everyone sees that material wealth acquired on earth, stays on earth.

3. I want my hands to swing in the wind, so that people understand that

we come to this world empty handed, and we leave this world empty handed, after the most precious treasure of all is exhausted, and that is TIME.

Are Our Days Numbered?

Scripture addresses the subject of time. Psalm 90:12, "Teach us to number our days that we may get a heart of wisdom." James 4:14, "What is your life? For you are a mist that appears for a little time and then vanishes." John 9:4, "We must work the works of him who sent me while it is day; night is coming, when no one can work."

I am haunted by the words of my college English professor long ago: "Some time is meant to be wasted." John Lennon is given credit for the quote: "Time you enjoy wasting is not wasted time." Maybe it's just me, but I always have felt a strong stewardship of time. Fishing, golf, television and table games always were relationship activities for me. You won't find me installing Christmas lights around the house because I enjoy doing it. Brenda has a beautiful Christmas spirit and I do it for her. What's wrong with that? Isn't it more blessed to give than to receive? Am I not to consider others as better than myself? (Philippians 2:3)

It is stunning to receive Father's Day and birthday cards from children and grandchildren with memories of time spent together. What we did together, stands out as a day in their history. It motivates me to step forward and create more. One day when I was five still looms in my memory. My maternal grandfather (visiting from Tennessee) took me to town on the bus and spent the day with me. I never doubted that I mattered to this good man. He likely had no idea that his attention would leave such a lasting impression on the small boy, who now has lived more years than he and carries one of his names.

In Mitch Albom's book *The Timekeeper,* we read, "Try to imagine a life without timekeeping. You probably can't. You know the month, the year, the day of the week. There is a clock on your wall or the dashboard of your car. You have a schedule, a calendar, a time for dinner or a movie. Yet all around you, timekeeping is ignored. Birds are not late. A dog does not check its watch. Deer do not fret over passing birthdays. Man alone measures time. Man alone chimes the hour. And, because of this, man alone suffers a paralyzing fear that no other creature endures. A fear of time running out."

My friend was right. Our hearts are drawn to something that is lost or didn't turn out the way we hoped. It is devastating to pour ourselves into the life of a child or grandchild, only to watch him/her make a life decision that leads to irreversible consequences. Nearby there are other precious lives and time is on our side—at least for a while. An adult choice is needed here. Mitch Albom also is right: "We yearn for what we have lost. But sometimes we forget what we have."

It was Barbara Bush who said "At the end or your life, you will never regret not having passed one more test, not winning one more verdict or not closing one more deal. You will regret time not spent with a husband, a friend, a child, or a parent."

The Message of the Firehouse

Pain hurts. There is no denying it. The things that bring hurt are not going away, as long as there is time. How do we survive and thrive? How do we get to the other side of the hurt and still be of value to others?

At age eighteen I arrived at the Naval Air Station in Atsugi, Japan, where I would spend two years. The leadership was big on fire prevention. Aircraft were in constant motion, even during the night. Soon after arriving, I walked by a miniature fire station on top of a pole placed along a walkway. On the front were the words "Open this door and see the number one fire prevention tool known to man." Unable to resist, I opened the door. Looking inside I saw my reflection from a mirror placed in the back. All my life I have accepted responsibility for my actions. There has been no one else to blame. How could I argue with the message of the firehouse?

I have made choices in life that brought pain to me, as well as others. There is no one to blame but me. A most treasured gift in my life is forgiveness.

However, forgiveness is like removing a nail. The nail can be removed but the hole remains. We can choose our behavior but not the consequences, and often they are lasting. The only place to turn is Christ, but we must take the first step.

Pain won't go away in this life. It is a challenge for me to join with David and say, "It was good for me to be afflicted so that I might learn your decrees." (Psalm 119:71) I'm still working on the directive from James: "Consider it pure joy, my brothers and sisters, whenever you face trials of many kinds because you know that the testing of your faith produces perseverance. Let perseverance finish its work so that you may be mature and complete, not lacking anything." (James 1:2)

Aesop said, "Better to be wise by the misfortunes of others than by your own." Isn't there a better way to learn? Does someone I love, need to accommodate me by suffering so that I can learn God's decrees and grow character in Christ? Who can argue with the fact that we come out on the other side of pain with character strength that would not come any other way?

C.S. Lewis wrote, "Hardships often prepare ordinary people for any extraordinary destiny." Everyone who has inspired me with their accounts of overcoming, has had a heavenly perspective and is very vocal about it. I'm not surprised. Lewis also wrote, "Aim at heaven and you will get earth thrown in. Aim at earth and you get neither." The apostle Paul wrote "I consider that our present sufferings are not worth comparing with the glory that will be revealed in us," (Romans 8:18)

This is a familiar quote by Charles Spurgeon: "A Bible that is falling apart, usually belongs to someone who isn't."

A message on the back of a t-shirt said, "Finish empty." What a great epitaph! It was the very thing Jesus said as He addressed the Father in John 17:4, "I have brought you glory on earth by finishing the work you gave me to do." The means of doing so might include playing golf with a lonely person, being available to someone struggling with grief, providing financial relief to someone who really needs it, touching the life of a student who is receiving little encouragement from his/her family or listening with our heart without offering advice or a comparable story.

My friend Joe Buzzello wrote the book *A Life in Sales*. He stated "Character is formed (and success is attained), when you run the long race. Are you willing to FINISH?" That worked for me in my own life in sales. I have established it as a priority in life as well.

Finding Strength

The Apostle Paul was on a mission and nothing discouraged him. He listed for the Philippians many of the hardships he endured to accomplish the assignment for which God had chosen him. Nothing mentioned was pretty, but he made the best of those challenges. He wrote from prison, "I have learned to be content whatever the circumstances. I know what it is to be in need, and I know what it is to have plenty. I have learned the secret of being content in any and every situation, whether well fed or hungry, whether living in plenty or want. I can do all this through him who gives me strength" (Philippians 4:11–13)

Wouldn't it be great at the end of your life to say confidently to God, "I have brought you glory on earth by finishing the work you gave me to do?" I can't think of a better legacy. Jesus showed us how and confirmed it to the Father. He is our model. I like the way *The Message* translates 1 John 3:2, 3: "All of us who look forward to his Coming stay ready, with the glistening purity of Jesus' life as a model for our own."

Paul's accounts give us a perspective that will carry us through life. I just know this won't plague us forever. "God shall wipe away all tears from their eyes; and there shall be no more death, neither shall there be any more pain: for the former things are passed away." (Revelation 21:4)

John Eldredge put it this way: "The human heart and soul are imbued with a remarkable resilience. But they are also very fragile, for we were made for the habitat of Eden and not the desolation of war in which we now live."

Death Changes Things

It was my second death call within a week. Coming home and finding her companion unresponsive on the floor, forced this person into unfamiliar territory. It's not a daily occurrence for anyone. Our lifestyle or expression of faith did not match, and I acknowledged that. I also acknowledged that the pain of separation was not foreign to me or the police officers that were with me.

A few days later, I conducted a funeral service for a grieving family facing a future much different than their past. Death is part of living in a world, after sin was introduced. (Romans 5:12) Death was not a familiar experience for Eve. That made it easy to believe Satan's lie when he said, "You will not die." (Genesis 3:4)

Grief is difficult, although it has value. In John Eldredge's book, *All Things New,* he writes, "The thing about grief is, it opens the door to the room in your soul where all your other grief is stored. Which can be a good thing if you handle it well, take the opportunity to heal the neglected grief. But still. Life begins to feel like it is only and always going to be loss."

What life "feels like" and "is" are two different things. Paul wrote, "The Lord is faithful, and he will strengthen and protect you from the evil one." (2Thessalonians 3:3) I believe it, continually experience it and observe it in the lives of those around me. This is my message to the hurting as I take one more ride.

Epilogue

During a routine visit to the oncologist, Brenda and I braced for the next step in her treatment. Instead, he told us she could stop her chemo. There no longer were any signs of cancer. About that same time, I came across a verse in my Bible reading—and I refuse to believe it was a coincidence. It was Ezra 9:8: "But now we have been given a brief moment of grace." Staci Eldridge wrote, "God drops things in our laps just at the right time."

Margaret Mitchell said, "Life is under no obligation to give us what we expect." If it's good news, what do we do with that "moment of grace"? Playing another round of golf didn't appeal to me. Surely, there was something better. Personally, I chose to take one more ride.

We went to the chemo room, hugged and thanked all the nurses who had provided loving care. They all lined up for a photo with Brenda. In the middle of the group was a large hand-drawn sign: "NO MO CHEMO." We still keep in touch with many of those nurses, have some over to our house and go to dinner with others. Brenda and I are not finished. Together, we have chosen to take one more ride.

A hero at the top of my list is my maternal grandfather. This man was orphaned at the age of fourteen with two young sisters. He took responsibility to get them accepted into an orphanage. They both grew up to receive college degrees and work for that same university until retirement. That account (and spending one day with this good man) instilled in me a heart for others.

On a visit to our home when I was five, Granddad took me to town on a city bus. It was just the two of us. On the sidewalk, he stopped and put money in a cup held by a monkey that belonged to a blind man playing the accordion. We stood and listened to the man play for a while. later I learned that Granddad's father was blind and played the accordion on the street. Granddad held the cup to collect money. I was moved by watching his kindness. It was a day that Granddad took me with him for one more ride.

Five months after his visit, we were in Tennessee. Two ministers conducting the funeral for my grandfather did their best to console a grieving six-year-old, as I was rotated from one knee to the other. A precious paternal grandmother suffering the effects of cancer was a brutal sight for a sixth-grade boy. Another classmate passed, then another and another. The rage at home due to Dad's excessive drinking added to the confusion. My brain could make no sense of it all. But, Leonardo DaVinci said, "Tears come from the heart, not from the brain." With years of searching for meaning and advancing years upon me, my heart was telling me to take one more ride.

I know I'm not the only one facing this dilemma. Nor am I alone in receiving benefits from the kindness of others. The search for purpose is a huge quest for any of us. It is something many never discover. I am persuaded that not a single one of us was put on earth merely to exist. Looking back at the tremendous feat of climbing Mt. Kilimanjaro with Parkinson's disease, R.W. Long stated his quest this way: "What purpose did it serve? With every question, there was the seeking of my Creator and, ultimately, the expression of the basic human desire to know why I was created and for what purpose."

In the back nine of my life, with an unknown number of days remaining, I know one thing for sure: living outside me is my sweet spot. I want to give back what I have received. I am thankful that I am married to a woman with the same spirit. Jesus said it; "It is more blessed to give than to receive," (Acts 20:35) No one can know the truth of this better than one who has received, and we certainly have. Holding the hand of someone experiencing trauma, brings immeasurable blessings to me and (I trust) to them as well. I am confident God will handle the results.

This effort is an account of discovery—the discovery of my purpose. It is set in stone for my remaining days. Through a lifetime of trial and error, the Heavenly Father has spoken. Clearly, He has invited me to take one more ride.

About the Author

Thomas Montgomery is a Navy veteran. He married Brenda three years after being released from active duty. That union has lasted 53 years. Tom received BA and MA degrees, in preparation for the ministry. After twelve years in full-time ministry, a career in the insurance field brought the couple to semi-retirement. Tom is adamant that he never left the ministry but built his business with his love for people rather than sales skills.

Tom and Brenda live south of Fort Worth, Texas, close to their entire family. The family includes three grown children, seven grandchildren and 4 great grandchildren.

www.ingramcontent.com/pod-product-compliance
Lightning Source LLC
Chambersburg PA
CBHW022007090426
42741CB00007B/931